ELA

A GREEK AFFAIR

ELA
A GREEK AFFAIR

By
Michael Saunders

EFSTATHIADIS GROUP

Efstathiadis Group S.A.
Agiou Athanasiou Street
GR - 145 65 Anixi, Attikis

ISBN 960 226 524 1

Printed and bound in Greece by Efstathiadis Group S.A.

To Pauline for her love.
For Hazel and Robert for their help
and for Georgette, Alekos and Roxannie
for opening my eyes.

Chapters

CHAPTER 1

A dream into reality

Oblivious to the sound of the taxi door closing, the lone figure of Stelios knelt at the end of the path. The man worshipped his garden, but complained continually of the work it involved.

"Yassou," I shouted.

With an effort he leant forward onto his forearms, like a sprinter gone to seed on his starting blocks. A backside slowly teetered into the air. With a grunting and a creaking of joints, he gradually raised himself to stand resplendent in a pair of baggy blue shorts and flip flops.

"Ti kanate," he beamed and the ebullient Greek strode towards us, arms held wide, trowel in one hand and a clutch of weeds in the other. "Welcome, welcome."

Stelios was in his late fifties with a totally bald head, which shone in the sun and a paunch on which much care and attention had been lavished over the years. He was never without a broad smile, or an infectious laugh and while he did not have a classical moustachioed features, he personified the true Greek hospitality - 'philoxenia'.

"Nice I see you again," he grinned, embracing Pauline, my wife -
"and you too Michylie."

Like a virginal forties film heroine succumbing to the charms of her leading man, I closed my eyes as he turned towards me. With arms limp by my side and eyes now puckered up tight with resigned acceptance, I stood my ground like a true Brit.

There was a pregnant pause. Then he kissed me. Twice.

I used to view this customary greeting of full blooded males with fear and trepidation. Today however, I can report I am fully experienced having kissed many men, and now pucker with the best of them - but only in Greece!

Our hellos over,Stelios mopped the top of his bald head and, with arms around both of us, we were steered towards the outside bar, resplendent under a roof of local bamboo, garnished with a fringe of gently swaying gourds. Stelios poured a welcoming drink. The first sip of ouzo anaesthetised my taste buds, but as the warm aniseed flavour gradually washed over my palette, I felt the journey drain away as I relaxed in the old wicker chair. With eyes closed I let my mind dance over the smell of basil and thyme wafting in from the garden and listened while the air filled with the staccato buzzing of cicadas in the olive trees.

We were back.

Stelios' pension lay in the village of Malame, some thirty five kilometres from Chania, in Western Crete. Made famous during the Second World War, by the famous Battle of Crete, the place was now firmly caught up in the tourism industry and boasted shops, tavernas, a supermarket and many places to stay.

Stelios had previously been an Officer in the Greek Navy, but on his retirement in 1985 had decided to build a new life and capitalise upon the growing tourist industry in this part of Crete. With an extrovert personality and a gregarious sense of humour, this larger than life character played the part of Zorba to the full. To tourists who owed no allegience to anything but the sun, he was an excellent host. To others, who felt there was perhaps something more to the country, he opened the door to a different way of life. These guests he looked upon as friends and took great delight in treating them to glimpses of the real Crete. Perhaps a special village celebration, way up in the mountains - an invitation to a wedding feast - or a Saint Day church service held just once a year in a tiny chapel no tourist could ever find on their own.

When not animatedly enjoying life, in his quieter moments Stelios would seek solace from the rigours of tourist entertainment by gardening. This would necessitate changing from everyday shorts and flip flops into gardening shorts and flip flops.

At this time of the year, in mid-September, the pension looked a picture, bedecked with magnificent purple bougainvillea. Surrounding the white square building were pots of all shapes and sizes containing sweet smelling gardenia and jasmine. A huge willow tree created a natural canopy of welcome shade beneath which guests could sit and sip a cool drink from the bar, just a few metres away. There was no bartender, you just helped yourself and recorded what you drank in a little book, settling up at the end of the week.

We had spent many holidays in this area of Crete, becoming enchanted by its people and captivated by the magnificent scenery. Now we wanted to buy a house here. Telling Stelios of our plans during a holiday the previous month, he had insisted on helping us. We agreed to return, when he had had a chance to make some enquiries. Now here we were.

As we sat, sipping our drinks, Stelios whetted our appetite with all the places he had arranged for us to see. Wishing to bring a little British formality to the occasion, I confirmed our willingness to pay a commission for his troubles. Like a scene from a Greek tragedy he was at once indignant that we could sully our friendship with money and then angry that we could dare question the regard his family and ours had for each other. Why, nothing would make him prouder than to know that he had been instrumental in finding a home where our children and their children could become true Greeks.

Stelios was surely as honest as the day was long - or were days just a mite shorter here?

The following day we assembled outside the pension and Pauline and I climbed into the back of Stelios' battered old Ford Escort Estate. The front passenger seat had long since fallen prey to an army of rodents and was now little more than springs and pieces of foam rubber. I nervously looked round to check whether any mice were hitching a lift. With only 21,000 kilometres on the clock - the second time around - he had bought the Ford at a bargain price of £7,000. Cars in Greece are extremely expensive.

Stelios' pride and joy had been re-sprayed in brilliant metallic red and featured a series of sensuous swirls on the side panels - za positive statement designed to reflect the owner's libido. Stelios had a reputation for being a ladies man - whenever his wife looked the other way - and viewed the car as an indespensible part of his seduction armoury. The Escort was his pride and joy, used in the foreplay of attracting admiring glances from potential conquests.

We hoped we wouldn't see anybody who knew us, while esconced in the back of this passion waggon.

Like cops on an emergency call out in an American film, Stelios reversed out of the driveway, into the direct path of an oncoming coach. Oblivious to the squeal of brakes and an ear shattering blast of a horn, he grabbed the gear knob - an acrylic encapsulated sea-horse - and threw the car into first. We jumped and hopped forwards, gradually gathering speed. Like some mighty ocean going liner sounding its fog horn, the doom laden sound of the coach signalled impending disaster. In fact the driver was so close, it seemed as if he had little option but to join us on board, via the back seat.

Thankfully the accelerating Ford outstripped the advances of the braking coach. As we picked up speed the coach driver obviously felt the need to impart a little advice to Stelios and pulled out to overtake.

It was a mistake.

At that moment, with crucifixes swinging wildly from the driving mirror, Stelios decided to turn left. He did so neither looking in his mirror, or signalling. As we disappeared up a tiny, dusty track, we heard a long screech of tyres as the coach skidded up the road. We prayed all the passengers would come to no harm.

We drove for maybe ten minutes past olive and orange groves, until we were astride the hills overlooking Malame and the Aegean Sea.

"Where could you see a better view than this? Ela - come".

Stelios threw open the door and was off, striding through the fields of vines. "Ela - ela," he called over his shoulder, as I battled to tilt the front seat forward sufficiently and extricate myself from the car.

We stumbled through the vines to where Stelios was standing, a raffia hat set rakishly on top of his bald head, for protection against the scorching sun. There was no question, the view was quite breathtaking. The coastline could be seen sweeping away into the distance, overseen by vast mountains: mere silhouettes in the shimmering haze. The blue of the sea, some ten kilometres away, appeared to merge into the cloudless sky, while below, everywhere was green with countless trees and bushes.

Stelios pointed to a large stone by our feet.

"Etho ...," and like a demented Basil Fawlty, proceeded to take large goose steps across the field, shouting out the number of paces as he went - "... stin etho. A good size yes?"

This Hellenic example of surveying, measured out a crude area of probably a quarter of an acre.

"Stelios," I called, "where is the house? We want to buy a house, not a field of grape vines."

"Just taste these grapes. Are they not the finest you have ever tasted," and he picked a huge bunch of luscious purple grapes as he made his way towards us.

"But we're looking for a house," I repeated.

"Oiki provlima," interuppted our guide, "just imagine the house you could build here, with such a fine scenery and such rich garden. Why I think you would have enough wine to drink for a whole year. I also think you will have many friends too."

"Imagine the cost of water. Imagine the cost of electricity. It will cost a fortune to run services this far out of the village," I countered.

"Precisely," nodded Stelios in agreement, his enthusiasm failing to be dampened. "That is why I have arranged for the price to be so low. Only four million drachmas."

"No, I'm sorry. It's not what we're really looking for," and I turned back towards the car. He was right though. The grapes were delicious.

We spent the next two days driving up mountains, down tracks and along beaches in search of the ultimate desires. At each site on his itinery, we would be treated to the same procedure. Screeching to a halt outside a tumble down shack, Stelios would wax lyrical over its hidden potential in such a manner that by closing your eyes to the derelict building in front of you, an architectural monuement of classical importance could be imagined. I swear the man must have taken a crash course in residential salesmanship. Only an estate agent would have the temerity to describe a tiny stone hovel, half way up a mountain, miles from anywhere, with two rooms, no roof, windows, running water, electricity or sewage facilities as - "This make you plenty money. You re-build this ancient home to former glory, just like our famous Acropolis."

We criss-crossed Western Crete looking at land we could buy, but not the olive trees upon it - a bamboo grove where a house would need stilts to keep it above the rising river in Winter - and a whole assortment of weird and wonderful monuments in bricks and mortar that provided man with refuge from the elements.

Back at the Pension we were beginning to get a little dispirited.

The ever enthusiastic Stelios was like a puppy dog, never failing to lose his enthusiasm over the next place he would take us to.

"Tomorrow I will take you to your house. It is so special. You will have the mountains and the sea together. I guarantee it."

That evening, over plates of kalamari, red mullet grilled to perfection, a Greek salad and fresh crusty bread, still warm from the baker's oven, we washed away our doubts over a Metaxa or two.

The following day, with an ever blue sky above us, we set forth again - this time with no adventures on the road. We headed Westwards along the coast through the next village of Tavronitis, towards the mountains in the distance. As we drove, it was evident the wave of tourism hadn't quite reached this far. People were in fields either side of the road, tending their tomatoes, cucumbers or melons. We overtook a man leading his donky, weighed down with horta, while an old couple chugged along at fifteen miles an hour, in what looked like a Heath Robinson contraption - half lawn mower, half buggy. Piled high behind them, huge water melons perched precariously, ready to bombarb any unfortunate pedestrian, whenever the vehicle lurched into a pothole.

After fifteen minutes we came to Kolimbari and turned off into the village. Brilliant white houses greeted us, as the curving, wide road narrowed into the main street. Men looked up from their games of tavli, others appeared not to notice as we sped past. Through the baker's open window we caught the intoxicating smell of freshly baked bread. Further on several people inspected a cart full of fresh fish for sale, landed early that morning. As we left the main street, we entered a tree lined avenue leading towards an old building some five hundred metres ahead. The road narrowed to such an impossible width, we thought we couldn't go any further.

"This is very old monastery," said Stelios, "there you can see icons which are six hundred years old. And there is the Acadamie. It is the most famous place in the world for studying our Greek Orthadox Religion."

As the old Ford squeezed past the studded doors of the old monastary, we could see ahead that the roadway led into a modern, churchlike building. As we approached at speed towards the wide open gates, we had a vision of buying a house with its own built in monastary. We were unprepared for Stelios turning the wheel and slewing the car round ninety degrees towards the sea to career down a road that had suddenly appeared to our right.

Gradually the road inclined upwards, with the mountain rockface on our left and below, to our right, the crystal clear blue sea. Ahead, an overhanging cliff had been half blasted away, leaving a narrow access for one vehicle. A musical blast on the horn warned everyone within five miles around that Stelios was going round the bend and would not stop for anyone.

As we sped along, I tried to take my eyes off the precious metre of road beside us. This afforded the only protection we had, from an enforced dip in the briny below. In a blase voice, which sounded a little too high pitched for comfort, I casually asked whether there was much further to go.

"Only four more kilometres," confirmed our all too cheerful driver, turning round to give me a broad smile, oblivious to the fact that we were rapidly approaching another bend.

Hypnotically I glanced down. Hell. It was a long way down. Had the road become narrower, or were driving closer to the edge? Forcing myself not to look at the stones casquading into the sea below, I looked upwards. God. Where were we going? The road appeared to go in a series of hairpins right over the mountain top.

With the engine roaring and Stalios cursing - or was it praying, he crashed the gear stick into a very unreceptive first gear as the roadway disappeared upwards and behind us.

"Ohh - just look at that." gasped Pauline, looking out of the back window.

Fully expecting to see a wheel bouncing down the mountainside, my breath was taken away by the picture postcard scene spread out far below us. A perfect shimmering blue sea lapped a ribbon of beach snaking thirty kilometres around a vast bay - studded with villages, each one clustered around its own domed church, while away in the very distance, hotels stood out, framed by a ragged backdrop of mountains soaring upwards into the heavens.

The moment was spoiled as we were thrown forwards - backwards.

Stelios had pulled his limousine up in the middle of fifty goats. A blast of the horn achieved nothing. The goats, all curly horns, floppy ears and long black coats, lazily sat down. Like seasoned demonstrators, they took up prone positions daring us to drive further up the mountain.

Being English, we would probably have got out and gently coaxed each animal out of the car's path, while we crawled along at two hundred metres an hour.

Being just a mite less patient, Stelios did things a little differently.

With a great deal of shouting and wild gesticulations out of the window, he revved up the engine, and, with horn permanently blaring, catapaulted the vehicle up the mountain road. Seeing he meant business and was obviously not a namby pamby tourist, the goats scattered out of the way.

Higher and higher we went. Suddenly around the corner came an old Toyota pick-up. Like a bat out of hell it was careering straight towards us. Before taking any necessary evasive action, it is obviously a local custom to insult one's neighbour before departing this world. In keeping with this tradition, they proceeded to hoot and shout obscenities at each other.

The driver of the pick-up then swerved away towards the mountainside. Stelios veered towards space and I closed my eyes.

With a great deal of screeching and swerving, both vehicles managed to continue their journies unscathed - unlike the passengers. This one in particular was extremely pleased to be sitting upon a tan coloured seat.

Upon reaching the mountain top, with the sea some seven hundred metres below, the road turned inland, leading us by fields of grape vines, grown so symetrically, the rows appeared to turn and travel with us. Above the vines were countless dusty green olive trees, while all around, mountain peaks surrounded us in a vast semi circle.

"My friends, welcome to Afrata," beamed Stelios.

Ahead, two rusty oil drums lay on either side of the road, to which were tethered two huge snarling dogs. Like a scene from Greek mythology, guarding the gates of Hades, these animals made sure goats would not leave the village. Unfortunately they also impaired the arrival of hapless tourists who chugged up the mountain on their rented scooters, only to run the gauntlet of snarling jaws, snapping at their ankles, as they gingerly edged past. Conditions were even worse for those intrepid walkers who braved the steep climb up from Kolimbari. Forced to keep to the middle of the road, for them the narrow path of safety was but a tightrope, fraught with danger. Edging fearfully forwards, a pace to the left, or a step too far to the right could leave a pedestrian not well versed in judging distances having to limp back down the mountain.

As we drove by the bullet marked sign for Afrata, with olive groves on either side, the road became potholed. Stelios did not once slow down, but twisted and turned the old car from one side to the other, in a vain attempt to miss the holes. Every third or fourth one would be too much for his rally skills and there would be a crunch from the axle beneath us and a clang from above, as our heads hit the metal roof.

Leaving the olive groves behind, we passed the old village church and came into Afrata itself. To the left, a tiny road led across the mountain to the next vilage of Rothapos. Above us, to the left and right, reached by a flight of stone steps painted in the palest of blues, were two Kafenios. Signs proclaiming that they served spaghetti, salads, drinks and coffee must be wonderful enticements to many a weary tourist. Especially those who had struggled up four kilometres of mountain, only to be savaged by two mad dogs.

There didn't really seem anything else here, apart from a couple of modern houses and two buildings which were only at shell stage. There was no time to ponder further, because Stelios was off again, down the tiny roadway to the right.

Incongruously a children's playground furnished with modern, brightly coloured swings and slides, was set amidst an olive grove. On our left, on a bend, was a house and outside was a perfectly preserved Mescherschimdt bubble car - but these were all impressions as we sped by.

And then we could see houses in front of us, with the road leading to a tiny village square. In Stelios' own inimitable style, we hit the square at sixty kilometres an hour, but, at the last moment swerved to the right and we carried on past and down a narrow lane. We could see tiled roofs and white painted old stone houses. Below us, villagers sat beneath the shade of grape vines growing above their verandhas. They glanced up at the sound of the battered Ford, but we were gone, leaving a vapour trail of blue smoke behind us.

Then the road ran out!

Thankfully, Stelios slowed down - albeit to forty kilometres an hour and we bounced down the steep, stony track, round tight bends, past homes covered in bougainvillea, set amidst wild gardens of fig, apricot, orange and almond trees, round which clucked hens pecking away at the remains of fruit, long since fallen.

Rounding the bend past the last house, we stopped. Stelios gestured with his arms held wide at the view below. "Here," he whispered, in hushed reverential tones, "is the house you always dream of."

I doubt it, I thought. I couldn't see anything except a thousand olive trees, out of which rose one, single Cyprus tree. Surounding us, the mountain ridge above tinkled to the sound of goat bells, while below, the chain saw buzz of cicadas filled the air. In a great 'V', the rocks and trees funnelled down into a deep gorge, and in the far distance the sea could be seen twinkling in the sun's rays. This was indeed a wonderful place - but to live here? I didn't think so.

My thoughts were broken as again the car charged down the stony track in a tornado of dust and flying stones. We hit the dip of a dried stream running across the roadway and ricochetted up the other side, slewing round to follow the downward track. Then, in a slurry of pebbles, we ground to a halt. We had arrived at our destination.

Our first impression was of total indifference.

A white wall, just over a metre high, completely surrounded the property. A blue gate with one hinge rusted through, granted access to a car port shaded beneath lush, green foliage heavy with grapes. A pathway scythed through a front garden of yellow, sun baked weeds and grasses standing a metre high. Twenty metres ahead, three steps led up to a raised verandha, edged by railings painted in traditional Greek blue. The house itself was rendered in a brilliant white and had an asbestos roof. It was 'L' shaped with faded blue painted window frames, inset with decorative wrought ironwork. Old shutters, warped in the sun, were too swollen to close, but nevertheless leant against each other to prevent sunlight from reaching inside. The roof overhung part of the verandha to create a shaded area of some four metres square. In the shade, out of the scorching sun, was a front door - a wide metal and glass affair.

With a great flourish, Stelios took a key from his pocket and opened the door. A pungent, musty smell escaped from the dark interior.

Once our eyes had become adjusted to the gloom, we could see that the floor was tiled. There was one rickety cupboard and a butler sink raised on wooden legs. A simple table and chairs were the only pieces of furniture in the room, apart from a built-in seating unit - the type with storage beneath. There was only one bedroom. It was tiny. A large brass bedstead had been squeezed in, which left no space at all for anything else. A huge lampshade hung down above the bed - a plastic carrier bag from the local supermarket, It ballooned out over the light bulb, creating an effective fly trap too, going by the number of prisoners it contained, and was a testimony to the owner's practical and innovative approach to interior design.

The loo would have qualified in the Guinness Book of records as being the smallest ever. It must have measured only one metre square, with a toilet, sink and a hole in the floor, for use as a combination shower room. I didn't doubt this was an excellent space saving idea in theory, but in practical terms, soggy loo paper fails dismally to meet the demands of an upset stomach. Reflecting this microcosm of bodily functions was a huge, decorative brass mirror, complete with candle bulbs and ornate filligree decoration. It wouldn't have appeared out of place in a church and almost demanded each enclaved visitor to cross themselves before partaking of the ablutions.

"This is perfect house for you and your family, no," queried our ever enthusiastic guide? "Just look at special design for much storage."

He bent down and lifted the seat to reveal the space below the seating unit. Six eyes blinked in the darkness. I blinked back.

Rats!

We made a swift exit.

"Pontikos is not problem," laughed Stelios, running out behind us, "we move them out. No need you be fright Paulina."

Paulina wasn't worried. It was Michylie who needed a chair to stand on and scream.

Outside, beneath the ancient olive tree in front of the house, Stelios waxed lyrical over our dream house. He then led us through a break in the boundary wall into the 'back garden'. It was a mass of weeds. but there were also four more olive trees, three orange, a peach, three lemon, a plum and two almond trees. A veritable orchard!

I could tell from Pauline's glazed expression that this place was beginning to exert a powerful hold over her. She wasn't seeing all the weeds, the dilapidated state of the house, or its sitting tenants. In her mind's eye there was a manicured lawn there, flowers here, wooden shutters at every window and comfortable patio furniture on the verandha.

I hadn't yet seen the light - only the hassle.

"I show you now why Afrata is, how you say, a duel in your crown." Stelios beckoned us out to the car. Again, we clambered into the back of the old Ford, sitting down with a jolt as the clutch was let out in a racing start. We hadn't driven barely fifty metres when, like a scene from the Keystone Cops, we stopped and, with an "ela, ela - come, come," from Stelios, we struggled out of the car just in time to see his backside disappear above us, as he ran up a flight of whitewashed steps set into the rockface.

At the top, a wrought iron gate swung open to reveal a concrete area beneath a huge rock overhang. In the mountainside was built a tiny chapel, bedded into the rock itself. Stelios untied the string wound round the door latch, serving as a lock, and crossed himself before stepping inside. We followed. The chapel was only four metres square, with an altar and on a table, several icons. An ornate unlit oil lamp was screwed into the rockface above us. In the corner was a bottle of oil and bread which was so old it looked like stone. In another corner, by the altar, were several pieces of metal, each one embossed, some with arms, others with legs or an eye. Stelios explained that when a villager had an ailment, they brought a metal plaque depicting the appropriate part of the body affected. By bringing it to the chapel, they believed the power of prayer would heal them.

If I could have found a little metal plaque of a bottom, I would have welcomed a few prayers to ease the effect of several days racing around Western Crete in the worn out seats and suspension of Stelios' passion waggon.

But, there was still more to see. Again we squeezed into the car and set off in a cloud of dust down through the mountain gorge. Huge boulders framed by gorse and barren rock stretched high above us. Mountain goats in impossible positions on the rockface, thoughtfully chomped on the sparse vegetation, while they idly observed the strange object with metallic red swirls emblazoned on its side careering away beneath them. Down we went and within four hundred metres we arrived at the beach! It was a tiny cove with a pebbly shore, only thirty or forty metres wide.

"See," beamed Stelios, "did I not tell you? Afrata is unique. It gives you the mountains and the sea."

I had to admit, that as far as Afrata was concerned, it was certainly a little corner of paradise. Three tiny fishing boats lay drunkenly on their bed of pebbles. The water, crystal clear, lazily lapped aginst the shore. We were the only people there, with the shimmering Aegean Sea in front and behind us, a backdrop of mountains rising directly from the beach. Looking up, I noticed a wire fence running the whole length of a ridge some one hundred metres above us. How strange I thought, and asked why anyone would feel the need to erect a fence in such an impossible position. The reason was simple.

"It's for the ships," confided Stelios.

Ships? There must be one hell of a high tide I thought. Then the drachma dropped. Sheep.

Bang on queue, with a clanging and a bleating, a whole flock of sheep appeared way above us. Down the mountainside they came with a shepherd behind them, whistling, shouting and throwing pebbles, cadjoling the flock into a controlled descent. Dutifully the sheep made their way onto the beach and passively filed into a rough wooden pen, built close to the shore. As the animals ambled by, I reflected that this was still only september. Where were the tourists? It seemed as if we were in a time warp, in a tiny part of Greece where life carried on the same as it had always done for centuries past.

If we were going to buy the house here, how much was it going to cost? Afrata was beginning to exert an influence over me which was beginning to feel irresistable.

CHAPTER 2

How much does a Grecian earn?

Stelios drove back up the steep track, past the chapel above us, the house on our left, round and up to the village.

"The owner, I think he live here," pondered Stelios, leaning over the steering wheel to look at a house with a wonderful shaded terrace. Winding down the window he shouted, "hey, Dimitrios - where are you? Failing to secure any reaction from the inhabitants, he got out of the car and strode onto the verandha, leaving us to wrestle with the seats and extrecate ourselves. By the time we caught up with him, he was eating some grapes, having helped himself from one of the luscious bunches peeping through the dense leaves shading the front of the house.

"Dimitrios. Ela na sou po ," bellowed Stelios in a voice so loud the whole village could hear.

A muffled voice from inside shouted a welcome to us and a few seconds later, Dimitrios shuffled out from the house. He was a tall man, in his sixties with a bulbous red nose and a paunch which strained his vest almost to breaking point. Straight, black hair was oiled tightly to his scalp. His eyes were hidden by tinted glasses, creating the impression of a Mafia heavy from a black and white 'B' movie, but when he smiled, his Grecian charm, and the effect of the Grecian 2000, transformed him into the look of a faded matinee idol.

"Yassus - katsi," welcomed Dimitrios and smilingly beckoned us to sit down at the table beside him. He offered us a cigarette, which we politely declined. "Anna. Etho," he wheezed and his wife appeared at the door, flustered, but smiling.

A short woman with greying hair and a smiling face, she bid us welcome. She was dressed in a bright summer dress and on her ample bosom wore several gold chains and a crucifix. The precious metal had a lustre to it as if worn by many past generations. Dimitrios addressed us in Greek, ignoring our smiles and vain attempts to stop him while in full flow. He didn't appear concerned that we couldn't understand a word he was saying. Suddenly a word leapt out of the conversation that I did recognise - coffee.

"Kafe? Parakalo," I said.

At this Dimitrios smiled and clapped his hands.

"Ah. You understand the Greek," said Stelios, very impressed. "How you like your coffee? Sweet, not so sweet or not the sugar at all?"

"Sketo," I smirked, deciding on the latter. Looking at Pauline to see how impressed she was by my linguistic ability, I received a fixed stare and her eyes rolled upwards - it spoke volumes as to my prowess.

However, my new friend was impressed and Dimitrios clapped me on the back and let forth a torrent of Greek. We were obviously going to be great friends now that we could both talk to each other in the same language!

A few moments later Anna brought out a tray, covered in a

lce doily on which were set five glasses of water and five small cups of coffee. Each reached out for their cup. Pauline politely sipped her coffee as if she were in an elegant drawing room. The two men noisily slurped theirs. It was something I had noticed before. Your purse your lips just above the coffee and suck up the hot liquid like a hoover, with almost as much noise. Well, when in Rome - so I slurped with the best of them. It was obviously recognised etiquette because nobody battered an eyelid. That is everyone except Pauline. I felt a lazer-like stare force me to glance in her direction. She looked at me horror struck and then her expression changed to the one every husband knows. The one that says 'you dare do that again and you're dead meat'.

Live life on the edge, that's my motto.

Having dispensed with the coffee and sipped at the water, Anna cleared away and brought out a tray of crystalised fruit. With much mimimg and cajoling, we were made to eat - a pear for me and an orange for Pauline. We rolled the fruit around in our mouths, biting through the thick, sweet syrup coating to the tart taste of the fruit. With our mouths full and our teeth stuck firmly together, we could only grimace and nod our heads vigorously in approval at how much we were enjoying these delicacies.

"Nero, parakalo," I managed to say, impressing my new friends even more with my linguistic ability. To many "bravos", I received another back slap from Dimitrios.

Thankfully the cool water which I had asked for, cleared our palettes. Not a minute too soon, for Anna then brought out a plate of almonds and sunflower seeds for our delectation.

"Now we talk business," grinned Stelios.

The two men talked incessantly, pausing only to make graphic comments with their hands. A shrug of the shoulders, raised eyebrows and outstretched palms obviously means the same in any language - "you can't be serious." Finally Dimitrios smiled and twice wiped his palms horizontally, the graphic sign that meant the subject of discussion was now at an end.

"I have worked very hard," said Stelios, obviously very pleased with himself. "Dimitrios will accept the offer I make for you. It is his daughter's house and because she lives in Athens, she has no need for a house in Afrata." He wrote a figure on a paper serviette - "it is a bargain, yes?"

I quickly attempted to calculate whether the buying price still appeared as attractive when converted into sterling.

Stelios interrupted my mental arithmetic.

"We have only one very small problem," and he held up his hand, pinching forefinger and thumb together, to demonstrate the extent of his concern. "For a foreigner to buy a house in Crete, he is able only to do this with a Greek partner. It is crazy i know, but it is for our country's defence."

He went on to explain that all the islands that lay on the frontier of Greek territory, was deemed a security risk.

"Does this mean we can't buy property here at all," Pauline questioned?

Stelios held out his hands and shrugged. "Greek law is like the circle. She go round and round with never an end," and he grinned - "but, there is always the back door we look for. You like this house? I believe there is not one finer in the whole of Crete. I, Stelios will help make it yours."

We hadn't discussed it but I could tell Pauline had already planned the building work to be done, right down to every little detail - probably even the colour of the curtains too. With a little imagination I must admit I was also sold. The price seemed reasonable - everything we were looking for and a sizeable amount of land too.

I looked at Pauline and she nodded in agreement. I confirmed the deal. "Yes Stelios, we love the house and accept the price."

Considering Dimitrios didn't understand English, he was very quick on the uptake when it came to money. Without waiting for a translation, he was shouting out to Anna to get something. Back she came two minutes later with another tray. This time five small glasses and a dish of peanuts in their shells.

"Ah, tskouthia," Dimitrios grinned, "Greek wheeesky. Penis?"

"Penis," I queried nervously? Was this a vital ingredient added during the distilling process? I peered at the crystal clear liquid in trepidation, not sure how, or why, a penis came to be in this drink at all.

"Penis," repeated Stelios. "It means you drink. If not 'penis' you will offend Dimitrios."

I took the glass which was offered, wondering what on earth was in the clear liquid. Lie back and think of England, I thought and spiritedly said, "yes, I penis with Dimitrios."

"No, no, 'penis' means 'you drink' in Greek. 'I drink' in Greek is 'penow'," laughed stelios.

I threw back the spirit and swallowed. My throat, my chest and then my stomach was set on fire. My lungs became paralysed and I fought for breath. Then taste and feeling gradually came back leaving a smouldering, warm taste that was really rather nice.

"What is it," I gasped?

Stelios laughed. "It is made in the village. After the grape juice is taken for the wine, all the remains they are boiled and make the smoke. Then the smoke she is made cold and turns into liquid - drip drip drip into a bottle. Ah. Tskouthia - and then penis?"

Everything seemed to be agreed, all except the question of ownership by a foreigner. Having said our goodbyes to Dimitrios and Anna, Stelios thought we should go to Chania and seek expert advice on how best to buy the house.

At seven o' clock the place was alive with tourists enjoying the atmosphere of the old Venetian town, while locals hustled and bustled about their business. Chania's main thoroughfare was thick with traffic, three lanes across. To our consternation, Stelios made it four, but not for long. He pulled up with a start and without a thought of the chaos created, leapt out of the car, leaving us to confront vehicles hooting and drivers shouting, as we struggled to get out of the car. With Greek oaths and an Anglo Saxon word or two ringing in our ears, we rapidly followed where we had seen Stelios go - up a flight of stairs leading to offices above the parade of shops.

On the first floor we found Stelios ensconsed in an office talking to an elderly man. The office was tiny to say the least, with room only for a large metal desk and two chairs. A shelf housed books and directories precariously balanced one upon the other, which rocked as the electric fan on the desk rotated within range. Posters of panoramic views decorated the walls, while everywhere plastic cups of half drunk coffee lay, stood, leant or balanced against piles of files.

"This is Stamatis," said Stelios, "he knows all things about the law. He is import export man. This is his company." He waved his hand around the shoe cupboard of a room, as if it was the headquarters of Olympic Airways.

Stamatis nodded towards us and then turned back to Stelios. The two then jabbered away, with arms flailing the air like two demented tick tack men at the Derby. Finally, Stelios shrugged and turned back towards us saying, "I think there is a problem. Stamatis say we should speak with lawyer. It is difficult, but there are ways to ... how you say ... get behind the law. Come. We go to fine lawyer. She speaks English, no problem."

With that we said our goodbyes to Stamatis and followed Stelios down the stairs into the warm night air.

Stelios walked as he drove - with isolated abandon. Waving us to cross the road, he strode into the traffic, which wasn't too much of a problem as the first lane was jammed and the second one was only moving slowly. It was the Kamikaze lane where it was necessary to possess a combination of lightening reflexes and devine intervention to reach the other side in one piece. Like Moses separating the Red Sea, Stelios cut a swathe through the traffic, without once breaking his stride.

Pauline and I were either too inexperienced or lacked Stelios' unerving belief in living to an old age.

We again went up another dingy flight of stairs, in an otherwise modern building. Like so many places we had seen, once the final stages of construction were underway, the builders fell prey to the Marie Çeleste syndrome, because invariably final cosmetic details would be missing. Wires would remain poking out of walls, floor tiling would end in a jagged edge, forever waiting for the final pieces to be laid. It is as if all the workmen are spirited away leaving empty coffee cups and newspapers littering the floor and the building is fated never to be totally completed.

We walked along the corridor past open doors until, three rooms ahead, we saw Stelios beckoning us into an office.

This was a solicitor's office?

Sat at a desk was the lawyer, a huge blancmange of a woman, holding court over eight people. She wore a matching twin set in pastel yellow, with two rows of pearls beneath her chins. This was most definitely not to be compared with traditional Dickensian solicitors in England, with all its hushed reverence and hushed privacy. This was Crete. Everyone shouted. The lawyer was dealing with three different cases at once - all the parties were in the same room. She would fire questions at one person, answer the telephone to deal with another problem and then resume dealing with another case from someone else in the room.

It was sheer chaos.

In his usual style, Stelios could not see the sense in waiting and began to address the solicitor with our problem. Repeating his initial question a little louder, but this time pointing to us as the obvious subject of his query, he caught the lawyer's attention. In perfect English she told us that the law was continually changing in Greece with regard to foreign nationals purchasing property there. This was especially so in Crete, which was recognised as being a sensitive area and necessary to the defence of the country's border. However, it was rumoured that by Greece now being a Member of the European Community, this law would be relaxed, but when - she shrugged - who knows? The only way to buy a property in Crete at this time, is to have a Greek partner. He would own the property, but a contract drawn up separately would confirm that we would have a vested interest in the freehold. This would prevent the property from ever being sold without our consent.

Then the telephone rang. With our query easily solved, she smiled, said goodbye and lifted the receiver to her ear and begun to concentrate on the call, which was no doubt far more interesting. Our problem, in her eyes had been solved and that appeared to be that.

Outside Stelios suggested we go for a drink and decide what to do.

Sitting at a harbour cafe, overlooking the sea, shimmering in the moonlight, with little fishing boats lazily swaying to and fro, it seemed absolutely imperative that we find a solution. The lovely village and tiny house had found a place in our hearts. Not to move there would be one of our greatest disappointments.

We stared at the water lost in our thoughts.

Solemnly Stelios cleared his throat. "I will be your Greek partner. I will buy your house and, of course, it will belong to you and your children. Before you go, you give me the money and I will make all the arrangements. No problem!

I knew this was not England, but nor was it cloud cuckoo land. Being used to the solicitors back home taking months to arrange searches, draw up contracts and cross every 'T' and dot every 'I', I did not believe this could all be done in the two remaining days we had left. We thanked Stelios for his help and promised to see him the next day to see whether we could finalise everything.

After he had gone, we sat for a further ten minutes watching the world go by, while artists beneath the harbour lights sold their wares of handmade jewellery, pottery, and pictures. We were due to meet our good friends Stavros and Mary for dinner, so, paying our bill, we mingled with the crowds strolling around the picturesque harbour and leisurely made our way to the Karnagio Taverna. This was one of the best places in town to sample excellent Cretan food and was patronised by locals and tourists alike.

We first met Stavros and Mary some six years previously. They own several jewellery shops in Chania and on our first visit to Crete we bought a few pieces there.

Pauline buys jewellery like she buys shoes, asking to see the whole shop in case she's missed something on display. From the complete stock review, a dozen or so options are then considered in more detail. The final contenders of two or three lucky pieces are then examined, tried on and fussed over. At last it is decision time. Invariably this results in buying more than one pair, because perhaps there could be a discount by purchasing more? This is all very well, but as Pauline finds it embarassing to raise the question, I am the one who has to negotiate in a vain attempt to try and claw back some of the over-spending.

Stavros is a goldsmith and comes from Athens. He has brown twinkling eyes, black hair and a beard, flecked with grey, a passion for backgammon and a low boredom threshold for anyone who cannot speak Greek. Mary is ten years younger and dresses impeccably as if she has just stepped from the pages of Vogue, her mane of black hair and olive skin setting off the exquisite jewellery that Stavros makes. With a clientel from all over Europe, Mary is fluent in English, German and some Italian and Fench. She is also a sound businesswoman, more than capable of holding her own, in the strong chauvenistic society of Western Crete.

When we first visited their shop, where Halidon Street mets the harbour, Mary invited me to sit and relax, while Pauline began her quest to try on everything in the shop. It was hard work. After half an hour I was offered a glass of freshly squeezed orange juice. An hour later up came a coffee. After many 'what do you thinks' followed by my grunts of approval, the selection was finally honed down to a gold bracelet and a pair of earings. At this stage Pauline became a chamelion and melted into the background. Behind, I could sense the hole in the ground opening up ready to swallow her as I began my 'what about a discount' routine.

For some reason, from that moment on, we all became firm friends - a friendship which, as the next few months were to prove, has grown ever stronger over the years.

Karnagio's is by the Custom's Office in the old harbour and is reached by a pleasant five minute walk over huge, irregular flagstones, set into the quayside. Fishing boats are moored cheek by jowl with beautiful yachts. Fishermen mend their nets on deck in readiness for the next tide, while the more well heeled enjoy aperitifs in their floating palaces. Round the harbour there are numerous tavernas and bars, past which crowds leisurely stroll, enjoying the romantic medieval atmosphere of one of the oldest, coastal towns in Europe.

Stavros and Mary were already at Karnagio's, with its forty tables set out in the warm night air. The taverna nestled at the foot of the spotlit stone walls of the old Custom's House and was packed with diners tucking into wonderful Greek and Cretan specialities.

Looking on and seeing more and more depressed the longer they had to wait, were a dozen or so people standing disconsolantly at the taverna's outer fringes. Like a game of chess, each party honed in on the particular table likely to be vacated next. Muscles tensed, poised to respond to a chair being slid away from the table. Yet at the same time , outwardly, each person attempted to put on an air of indifference as a decoy to thwart the others. We had seen this approach adopted by tourists many times before - all to no avail.

A local family will arrive, ignore the dithering novices and walk up to friends they know and join them at their table. All spare chairs are commandeered from around the taverna to seat the new arrivals, much to the chagrin of those still waiting.

As we approached the taverna, an English tourist waiting for a table, believing we were comrades, confided there was a half hour wait. With "hey. Wait your turn. Bloody germans," ringing in our ears, we walked through the tables to where our friends were sitting.

Never one to wait, Stavros had already ordered our meal. A Meze starter with small dishes of fried cheese, kalamari, fried auborgine slices, teropitta - small filo parcels of feta cheese -

and grilled octopus. While we tucked into the appetising food, washed down with local wine, we told Stavros and Mary what had happened that day. Between mouthfuls, Stavros would interrupt - "Ti?" or "Pos?" - and then Mary would have to recount the day's events. By the time the main course arrived, of Greek Salad and a huge grilled fish, garnished with lemons and potatoes, Stavros had the whole story.

"Oiki provlima," he muttered. "Signomi," and continuing to speak to Mary in Greek, he patted her arm and made his way to the back of the taverna.

"Please excuse Stavros," said Mary, "he is going to find out a little more."

Mary couldn't understand why we were so drawn to Afrata, already talking as if we lived there. The fact was, we were totally committed. Somehow, despite being there for no more than an hour or two, we had discovered a magical place you could only ever find at the end of a rainbow. Our good fortune was not so obvious to Mary.

"It is village," she grimaced, "why do you not prefer a house here in Chania? Afrata is so quiet. People only die there."

Even though she came from Kolimbari, the village near Afrata, Mary far preferred the town. She thought nothing of flying across to Athens for a hair appointment, or to shop there for clothes. When the tourist season ended, in October, she Stavros and their two boys would invariably fly to Italy for a long holiday and spend Christmas and New Year in Austria. Such a lvish lifestyle was not quite in keeping with the simplicity we had fallen in love with at Afrata.

Stavros returned to the table with an angry frown on his face.

Something was obviously wrong.

He sat down and proceeded to rattle off staccato sentences to Mary in Greek. By her expression and his hands animatedly conducting the air, we knew that something was most definitely not right.

After what seemed an age, Mary placed a restraining hand onto Stavros' arm to bring the tirade to a halt. She then brought us up to date with what Stavros had discovered. The house in Afrata had been advertised in the local newspaper. The advertisement read -

SMALL VILLAGE HOUSE WITH SERVICES AND NINE OLIVE TREES. INCLUDES LIVING ROOM, BEDROOM AND BATHROOM. TELEPHONE KOLIMBARI 824.

It then listed the price - some two thousand pounds cheaper than Stelios had told us!

Locals knew that Stelios had hoped to build a swimming pool at his Pension. Bank rates were sky high and the two thousand pounds would have been a great help.

There was more.

Stavros had actually telephoned Dimitrios, who confirmed that the English couple would get round the law by Stelios being their Greek partner. In effect, we would be paying Stelios the money and he would arrange to make the purchase. Later, he would have a letter drawn up, confirming that we owned the house with him. We were flabbergasted. Being in business ourselves, we felt we knew how to sum people up fairly accurately. This time we were miles out. Stelios was so likeable, so helpful AND we had even offered to pay him a commission!

Stavros then went on to say that he had persuaded Dimitrios to lower his original price by 500,000 drachmas. He had asked Stavros to tell the Englishman that he, Dimitrios, was proud of his country and would be pleased if we would take coffee with him and his wife the next time we came to the village.

The next time! We were returning home the next evening. There was so much to arrange. Buying a house in Greece was altogether a far more different proposition than in England. Our good friends Stavros and Mary came to the rescue again. Everything would be no problem. They would arrange for their lawyer to check over the deeds and a surveyor to register the land title. Being a village house, boundaries were often marked by nothing more than a few stones, a tree and a few stakes in the ground. It therefore made sound sense to have the land accurately surveyed. If we trusted them, they would have the deeds drawn up in Stavros' name and when the law was eventually changed - as was normal with every law of this kind - they would assign the freehold to our children, thus saving a payment in property transfer tax. On asking when the lawyer would require the money, Mary laughed. The lawyer wasn't buying the house. We had to give the money to Dimitrios, but this also was no problem. Stavros had sufficient money. We could bring the money over next time we returned to Crete.

"But that won't be until next May," I said, overwhelmed at their generousity.

"No problem," came the reply.

It was certainly not the way things were done in England. Nevertheless upon our return we immediately arranged for the money to be transferred bank to bank. It took three weeks for the funds to arrive in Stavros' account.

We discovered later that four days after we had left, Dimitrios had come down to Chania, dressed in his best suit, with a plastic supermarket bag. Stavros gave him the money in cash and, clutching his 'shopping', he caught the next bus back to the village. The house was ours.

CHAPTER 3

The Greeks have a word for it

Having arrived home from our house hunting exploits, we decided a committment had to be made. We didn't want the villagers to think of us as tourists, regally descending upon them every Summer. We wanted to be accepted and become part of the village community. To do that, we had to learn their language - and apart from anything else, nobody spoke a word of English!

With the decision made, we enrolled at the local college. The course was a one year's City and Guilds in Modern Greek. From then on, at seven o'clock evry Wednesday, we were to go through hell and back.

There were twenty eight of us who stood hesitantly in our alloted classroom at that first lesson. As the clock tolled seven, so our tutor swept in with greetings of "yassus, yassus. Katsi, katsi." We looked at each other - what did she say?

"Please," smiled the tutor, a wide theatrical sweep of her arms indicating that the furniture in our midst did have a purpose.

Like obedient little children, as one, bottoms instantly dropped onto plastic chairs set behind wooden tables, serving as desks. God. How the years came flooding back. Detention. Lines. Having to see the Headmaster for some misdemeanour.

I looked around my seated classmates. Who would be teacher's pet? Who would be the class swot? Who would be the dunce? I took comfort that the innocent were unprepared. Many had failed to bring a pad and pencil. Being a teacher's pet in the making, I had had the forethought to bring along a ring binder, pen AND a Greek dictionary. I sat smugly with arms folded while teacher called the register.

We were each asked our name and told to be sure and keep the same seats every week, in order for our teacher to remember who was who. As each person gave their name, they were christened with the Greek equivalent. When it came to my turn, I called myself Michylie. The fixed stare I was given clearly marked me down as being far too clever for my own good. I had already blotted my copybook and we hadn't even started yet.

The pupil beside me was from Bangladesh. His name was Chundra, but christened in Greek he became Vaseeli. I smiled at the exotic racial cocktail. As I was to discover later, in future lessons, Chundra wrote down his Greek and translated it firstly into Urdu, before copying the final version into English.

Having noted all our names, the tutor then stood to introduce herself.

"Kali spera, eemai Georgette," and she wrote her name in Greek on the board behind her. "I shall try to remember your name, please try to remember mine."

This simple fact was to be indellibly seared into our minds during the second lesson. Phil, a friendly soul, had a query. Attempting to draw our teacher's attention, he committed the cardinal sin.

"Georgina," he called?

No response.

"Georgina," he repeated a little louder?

This time she did hear. The verbal lashing Phil received over his mistake, made even Chundra blanche. From then on nobody ever forgot her name again. To this day I am sure Phil occasionally wakes at night trembling with the memory of that fateful day.

Georgette was a lady of indeterminate years. Her carefully coiffed fair hair, stylish dress sense, Pierre Cardin glasses and Gucci shoes, epitomised that continental flair for elegance and sophistication.

Greek by birth, to a family well known in Athenian society, she had lived in the capital until her marriage to an English army officer, forty years ago. Although raising a family and having lived in England longer than in Greece, in her heart Georgette was still very much Greek, with a personality truly relecting her Hellenic ancestry. She could at once charm and in the next second, if affronted, could become a dragon whose unleashed firepower, had already been felt by poor old Phil. Yet beneath, there was always a soft marshmallow centre of kindness.

It quickly became obvious to me, that if I was going to survive the difficulties of wrestling with the Greek language, then I had to make pretty damned sure I appealed to Georgette's softer side.

After one particularly difficult lesson it was evident I needed to call upon additional rescources to help smooth my way into

Georgette's good books. What better than the classic solution for cementing good pupil, teacher relations? An apple!

The very next lesson I arrived with my gift. Laying it on her desk, I said "echo ena milo yia tin thaskala - I have an apple for the teacher."

I didn't actually have an apple, but the bottle of ouzo more than made up for the fact.

In fact, as we have come to know her more, a close friendship has developed. One which we value for its warmth and openess, typifying so much the Greek committment to friends.

The lessons started with learning the Greek alphabet. With only twenty four characters to learn, that was the good part. The bad part was the confusion. A Greek 'n' is an English 'v' and an English 'n' is a Greek 'i'. It gets worse. Having grasped an 'n' in Greek, it is pronounced 'i', the capital equivalent in Greek is 'H'. There's more. An English 'p' is a Greek 'r'. Would we ever make it through the exam?

Weeks went by and the first flush of holidaymakers who wanted to learn Greek after a package fortnight to Corfu, began to drop out. A couple of weeks further on and the two girls who had fallen in love with Greek waiters, discovered absence doesn't make the heart grow fonder and their romance floundered - and so did learning the language. Three months into the course and twelve stalwarts remained.

Then, one Wednesday, in walked Brian.

"Sorry I haven't been before, but I'm on nights. There's no problem. I'm a quick learner. I'll soon catch up. Can you give me some homework to take as I can only get here once every three weeks, because I'm on shiftwork."

The man's either a benious or a fool, I thought.

Georgette obviously thought the latter.

Suffice to say, he never turned up again.

The courageous few battled on. We hit Christmas stuffed full of genetive, accusative and nominative cases. Come january, when we all reassembled, we were down to the final eight.

Like athletes training for the Olympics, we limbered up with a few verbs and ran through our paces of what to expect in the exam. Apart from the daunting terror of having to conduct a conversation in Greek for thirty minutes, there were four subject areas to cover. Firstly we would exchange pleasantries, secondly we had to name the objects in the examiner's handbag, thirdly we had to answer questions on an illustration and the last fifteen minutes - a lifetime - we had to talk about a picture or photograph of our own.

As the exam loomed ever nearer, so my grasp of the language seemed to diminish even further.

Georgette held her exercise book on her hip like an armed terrorist, with her Kerachnikof cocked. Taking aim, she would fire questions at us and we would blink like bunnies caught in the headlights of a car.

That is, all except Frank. No matter what was asked, he had the answer, reacting like lightening to every question that was fired. Frank was German, whose approach to life was akin to perpetual mourning. He was totally commited to not only passing the exam, but passing it with distinction. Consequently he was always to be seen around town on his bike, with clipboard fastened to his handlebars. Wherever he went, Frank studied. The problem was, that even though he had tremendous vocabulary, he spoke with such a gutteral accent, that nobody could understand him.

However, he was not to be daunted. I unfortunately had to spend a whole lesson pretending to listen intently to him describing a picture of a house. He knew many useful and often-used words, indispensible when conducting a normal everyday conversation. Words like - seamless guttering and portico! He was brilliant. The man would pass the exam with flying colours. There was no doubt he had the ultimate secret weapon. Put him in front of the examiner and he would surely gain a pass, conditional only that he left before she died of boredom. In fact, when describing his picture he went over the allocated time. On being asked to stop, he told the examiner that as he had studied for many weeks on this particular item, he would be pleased if she would do him the courtesy of letting him finish - and he carried on for another boring five minutes, depite attempts by the examiner to shut him up.

You will be pleased to know that Frank merely gained a pass. However, with true Teutonic dedication he re-sat the whole thing the following year in order to gain a distinction. He is now studying Italian and Spanish - the only man to speak fivelanguages all sounding the same.

Evening class was two hours every week, but, with the exam getting closer and the pressure building, the need to cram in more and more information became ever more urgent as I tried to compensate for the vocabulary that I was forgetting.

The big day at last arrived. Like school children, we arrived at the college clutching the pictures on which we would have to conduct a conversation. As each victim came out of the torture chamber, the petrified remainder would vainly attempt to monitor whether any questions were being repeated. Just before it was my turn, I received a valuable piece of information. The examiner had a knife, fork and spoon in her handbag.

Panic.

What was it - makairi - perooni - kootali. What the hell did this mean. I had revised the vocabulary perfectly - make-up, comb, lipstick, but cutlery? What sort of woman went out with a knife, fork and spoon in her bag? Obviously someone who likes her food.

What was it again? Too late. My name was being called.

The examiner was not how I pictured her at all. She hid her fetish for opportunist eating extremely well. She was in her thirties, slim, very attractive with a mane of black hair, and was dressed in a purple suit and wore an enchanting smile.

Unfortunately, when she spoke I couldn't understand what she was saying. The early years of learning my arithmetic tables at Primary School came flooding back.

"Saunders! Seven eights!" My mind, like now, would be a complete blank. I stared into space hoping that answers would appear. Again she spoke. Nothing. How on earth do you crank start your mind in this situation?

Eureka!

"Signomi," I asked, remembering that 'excuse me' was a tactical way of playing for time. Asking for the question to be repeated, gave me the opportunity to pull out the choke start to my brain. Again, nothing. This time she repeated the question in English. Like a kickdown on the accelerator, I opened my mouth and out came Greek. We were off.

Naming the colours of her scarf was easy. Opening the book at the right pages to demonstrate I knew my numbers was OK. Reading too wasn't a problem.

Then came the dreaded handbag.

Lipstick - crayon. Correct.
Watch - roloi. Correct. Face Powder - pouthre. Correct.
Mirror - kathreptes. Correct.
Diary - agenda. Correct.

And that was it. Not a sign of the sodding cutlery!

The examiner then looked through several magazine pictures and selected one. It was an advertisement with four scenes depicting lounge,bedroom, bathroom and kitchen. Immediately I sensed problems. Did I have sufficient vocabulary - and if I did, would my memory decide to go walkabout?

First question. Something about the lounge. "Signomi?" Something about the lounge. What was she saying? And then pure inspiration. Holding the page out at arm's length and squinting, I said in perfect Greek, "excuse me, but I have forgotten my glasses and I can't really make the picture out."

With that the examiner was kindness herself. She described each scene, which gave me time to think and concoct some semblance of an answer.

The final fifteen minutes was down to the photograph I had brought in with me. It was of the house in Afrata. I had spent weeks revising phrases and luckily I remembered them all. Consequently I was able to converse and answer all the questions the examiner threw at me - and then it was all over.

I staggered out into the foyer, like a prisoner savouring his first taste of freedom. Now all that remained was to wait for the result.

Four weeks went by and then the dreaded day arrived. A small brown envelope popped through the letterbox. Inside was a yellow form. At the top was printed City and Guilds Examination in Modern Greek. Each section of the exam had been marked individually with a tick in one of the colums - distinction, credit, pass and fail. At the bottom was a total.

I had passed.

CHAPTER 4

Everything is OK - no problem

In the September, before leaving, we had discussed with Stavros the structural changes we wanted to make to the house in Afrata. The existing bedroom was far too small, so we decided to build a second by utilising the 'L' part of the verandha. The unit with the rats would be cleared and the window above was to be enlarged to create a new front door. The miniature bathroom would be totally removed, to give a larger lounge and kitchen area. A door, put into the rear wall, would lead to a brand new bathroom extension. New floor tiles were being laid throughout, a kitchen fitted and all the windows would have new wooden shutters.

Throughout the winter months we had written and telephoned Mary to check on the progress being made.

Now, here it was July and we were on our way to Crete.

In our luggage were things even the most discerning of tourists would never dream of carrying. Picture frames, electric kettle, shower curtain, lamp shades - everything except a cuddly toy. And in the hand luggage? The piece de resistance - a cooker! Also, in our main case, wrapped in blankets was a special gift for Stavros. A token of our thanks for his help in overseeing all the building work.

Life is never easy.

While air traffic controllers across Europe layed down their computers in a quest for more money, we began our journey ground to a halt for two days at Gatwick Airport. Eventually, common sense prevailed and we said a fond farewell to the green chairs which had served as bed and lounge for forty eight hours and made our way to the Departure Lounge.

Now, at long last, after three and a half hours flying time, all the delays and inconvenience flew through the window as I looked down to see the runway rushing up to meet us. A jolt, a bump and a roar of engines heralded our arrival at the tiny airport of Chania. In the early eighties, landing there was a little like arriving at a second world war landing strip, edged by misson huts. Now, though small, but very much updated, it serves the package holiday arrivals to Western Crete.

The short walk across the tarmac led to a queue outside the terminal building, which slowly sifted through passport control towards baggage reclaim. Two hundred people jostled for pole position, while to the rear, others stood guard over their partner's hand luggage.

Meanwhile outside, on the tarmac, a lone figure stood by a crocodile of carts watching a companion leisurely disembowel the aircraft of cases.

Inside, all eyes were transfixed on the little door at the end of the carousel. Ears were attuned to the sound of machinery being switched on - but there was nothing to be heard. The minutes ticked by. The heat began to build and bodies began to perspire, leaking from every pore. Still the carousel remained doggedly motionless.

Back at the plane, activity had slowed to a snail's pace. After all, there were still another eight planes to arrive that day and baggage handlers had to pace themselves for the rush. Nearly an hour had passed, but finally a convoy of carts were now piled high with cases.

Back at the Terminal, cries from sharp eyed observers reconnoitering the lie of the land, signalled the baggage was coming. The information galvanised everyone into action. The chug of the carts drawing up outside could plainly be heard. The conveyor cranked into action. Grunts and wheezing signalled cases were being manhandled. A loud creak from rusty bolts being drawn back was met by raucous cheering from the otherwise phlegmatic Brits. At long last the door swung open to reveal the first case, wobbling into view. Everyone took up start positions - legs apart - body at right angles to the conveyor - grab arm held out at thirty degrees - the traditional stance of the holidaymaker hunting for his luggage. Eyes remorselessly scan every object on the carousel, as it comes through the hatchway, mentally discarding those of alien shape and colour, which does not comply with the specification lodged in their memory bank. When a hunter spots his prey, he tenses, motionless. Come the moment, he pounces with perfectly timed animal grace, snatching, lifting, swinging and turning the case in a perfect arc, scything it through the gaggle of inquisitive children at the front and weaker stragglers standing behind, as he and his party make their quest for freedom.

After the first surge of luggage, there is always a lull. This is when the cardboard box appears.

In every airport, all around the world, there is always a corrugated carton, complete with stickers, which travels round and round between each carousel fill-up. Nobody, anywhere, ever lays claim to it. Why is it there? To serve as entertainment value during an interval, like the potter's wheel of old, on the BBC? Or is it some sort of minimum weight requisite, necessary to maintain conveyor movement?

Against all odds our luggage was one of the first in line from the second wave of cases loaded onto the carousel. Feeling exposed without the protection of other fellow travellers, we inched our way as inconspicuously as possible towards the exit. The walk between the two Customs tables was the final hurdle to freedom. With cropped hair, heavy jowls and as much sex appeal as a Russian hammer thrower, a uniformed woman Customs Officer stood, with arms crossed, surveying the mottley crew shuffling towards her. Like a baggage x-ray machine, her piercing eyes scanned us intently.

"Stamata!"

Our blood froze. She was talking to us.

"Yassus," smiled Pauline innocently, "me theleis na anigo tis valitses mas?"

I couldn't believe it. My wife had actually asked, "do you wish us to open our cases."

Delighted that someone from this foreign plane was civilised. the Officer smiled - or to be more accurate - she grimaced, and replied, "Ah. You speak little Greek. What you have in the case, for she looks so heavy. Maybe you have in there, a computer, yes?" We all laughed at the joke and she waved us through.

Little did she know. We glanced at each other. Our gift to Stavros was safe.

Outside there was a throng of tour representitives, a queue of bronzed holidaymakers checking in for their return journey and a whole car park full of coaches, taxis and hire cars. Amidst the melle stood Stavros and Mary, looking a little apprehensive. It seemed there were just a few finishing touches to be made to the house. Nothing much, just a matter of a day or two. No problem. We were to stay at a pension near Kolimbari, owned by a friend of theirs.

The Pension was superb. It was brand new and really comfortable. Quickly unpacking, we joined our friends for a drink, at the taverna opposite. Over an ouzo they explained building work on the house had had to wait until the end of January. With the grape and olive harvests lasting until the end of January, families in the villages all had to work together to pick their crop. Then there was the rain. This delayed things. And then the tourist season began at the end of March, and everyone knew building work was difficult to rush in the Summer. Stavros had been to the house continually - sometimes three and four times a week, but it had been extremely difficult to dovetail everything together, as individual village tradesmen had been used. Nevertheless, we were to stay at the Pension, as their guests, over the next day or two when everything would be finished and we could then move in.

Impatient to say the least, once Stavros and Mary had left, we immediately arranged a hire car and headed towards Afrata to see for ourselves exactly what progress had been made on the house. It was now six o'clock. We had a couple of hours before dark.

When we arrived, while there was no front door - just the opening - we were pleased to see the new bedroom had been completed, but there didn't appear to be much activity. Tentatively looking into the loungs, we were relieved to see the floor tiles had been laid, but our hearts sunk - there was no kitchen. Worse. While the new bathroom's floor and walls had been beautifully tiled, there was no loo, sink or shower. In fact there wasn't a sign of any plumbing whatsoever. There didn't seem any chance at all of the house being finished during our short, two week stay.

Dejectedly we went outside and sat beneath the knarled old olive tree. The sound of tinkling bells in the olive grove on the land next to ours, heralded the arrival of a flock of sheep. The delicious chocolate taste of fallen fruit from the carob tree had attracted them. While the animals foraged by the fence, a distant voice calling the sheep, grew closer. At eye level you can only see dense foliage as the olives appear to grow into each other. Bend down and the scene is like an aeroplane descending through mist into clear blue sky. At waist level, the clouds of dusty green leaves gave way to the view of a two acre field, punctuated by twisted trunks. Walking purposefully towards the sheep was a little old man with a shepherd's crook. He must have been about seventy, slim, with a ram-rod straight back and the sauntering swagger of a man many years younger. He wore baggy trousers with boots and a blue Olympic Airways shirt. Beneath a thick head of curly white hair, glasses were perched on the end of his nose, above a clipped moustache. Seeing us, he appeared a little unsure. What were tourists doing here, trespassing?

A cheery "yassus," appeared to reassure him. In faltering Greek we tried to explain that we had bought this house. With a smile of appreciation at the attempt we were making to speak in his language, he introduced himself as Alekos, saying, "it would give him great pleasure to buy us a coffee at the Kafenio, which he and his wife owned. However, he must first water the sheep. He would see us in one hour's time." With that he was gone, bounding over a dry stone wall like a mountain goat, calling "ne, ne, ne." Dutifully the sheep followed.

We were extremely pleased with ourselves on being understood - and, even better - to understand, after a fashion, what was being said. Then we returned to the dismal prospect of not being able to stay at the house this time around. However, just sitting there, with the sound of silence filling the air, beneath the mountains towering above us, we had no doubts. This was indeed perfection.

Leaving our car beneath the canopy of vines, heavy with unripened grapes, we walked up the steep track towards the village above us - a leisurely stroll of no more than six hundred metres. The incline began to bear down on our ability to breathe. Steps became shorter and stops became longer as we made our way ever onwards. Like aged marathon runners we arrived at the Kafenio gasping for air.

Outside, beneath a huge tree, sat three old men sipping coffee. Hearing the puffing and panting of two unfit foreigners, one of the men called out, "Roxannie - ela." An elderly woman came running excitedly out of the Kafenio. "Yassus, yassus," she smiled in welcome, pulling chairs out for us, "katsi, katsi." We gratefully collapsed on the wooden chairs, feeling the wicker seats begin to create a lasting impression on the backs of our thighs.

Roxannie was probably about sixty, with thick, steel grey hair and a laughing face framed by glasses with thick lenses. She wore a simple grey dress covered by an apron and a gold crucifix hung from her neck. Having made sure we were settled, she turned and ran to the corner of the square, with an effort which appeared to trigger a miriad of painful afflictions. "Cleo," she shouted, "etho parakalo." The instruction ran round the mountains and returned. Wherever Cleo was, she would hear.

Roxannie's voice would put a Town crier's to shame. The Kafenio had virtually the only telephone in the village. When it rang, she would answer it and dash into the square to call out the name of the person needing to come to the 'phone. Within seconds, someone would be shuffling along to receive their call.

Roxannie never, ever took things slowly, even though she was a martyr to suffering, continually finding an ailment here and a searing pain there. We were to discover this cross she had to bear was a constant source of joyful banter from her nearest and dearest.

Walking back towards us, she grimaced, holding her hip and limping with pain. Concerned, I helped her to a chair, in which she slowly sat, her eyes tightly closed and hand to furrowed brow. Slowly, with effort, she recounted the terrible day, eight years ago, when the donkey fell on her. I bit my lip. The locals were less restrained. Guffaws and a great slapping of thighs greeted this sad tale. The play for sympathy now over, Roxannie turned and shouted something unintelligible which served only to fan still more laughter. Seeing my unsuccessful attempt at compassion, her face broke into a grin. Slapping me on the arm she proceeded to tell me what a naughty little boy I was and gave me a huge hug.

In the midst of all this jocularity, a pretty girl of seventeen came running round the corner. This must be Cleo. Introducing herself in excellent English, she explained that Roxannie and Alekos were her Grandparents. Apparently nobody in Afrata spoke English, apart from some of the children who were learning at school. We explained we had bought the house below the village. Cleo laughed. This was a small community and it was already common knowledge. She told us our house was in an area known as 'Ligari'. When asked what this meant, she replied it was named after a flower which was quite rare on Crete. Apparently it had a spiky mauve bloom, which attracted many butterflies.

At that moment Alekos appeared, mounted on a mule. Like a character out of some moussaka Western, he swung out of the uncomfortable looking wooden saddle and strode towards us, arms extended in welcome. Shaking our hands, he asked Cleo if we would like coffee. To show my prowess, I looked towards the three men and shouted across in Greek, "would you like a drink?" They just stared and said nothing. Thinking they didn't hear me, I repeated the question. Still no response. Cleo giggled and asked me to translate my question into English. Her giggles turned to laughter. What I had actually said was, "what are you saying?" She explained that in Greek it was important to emphasise the stress on each word, otherwise I could be saying something with an entirely different meaning!

My stumbling Greek broke the ice. When told the joke, everyone laughed and Roxannie slapped me across the back and pinched my cheek.

"Torra, tha sas thino ee kafess," she chortled and scooted off to make our coffees.

Alekos pulled up a chair beside us. Through Cleo we explained that we had hoped our house would be finished by now, but it didn't appear to be the case.

"There is no problem," confirmed Cleo, "my Uncle builds your house and he says everything will be finished in two days. You must rememember, this is Greece. Do not worry."

We sipped our coffee, chatted and ate the fruit which Roxannie kindly brought us. Then, as the sun went down behind the mountains and dusk fell, we bade farewell and, with our new friends waving, we set off down the stony track, back to the house. This time the excercise was less demanding, but the view was just as breathtaking as we strolled along. The only sounds to be heard in the still evening air were our footsteps on the rocky path and the tinkling bells from the mountain goats as they jumped from crag to crag. In the far distance the hoot of an owl and the bleat of sheep punctuated the vast stillness.

"Look," pointed Pauline, "These flowers. They are the ones Cleo was talking about - called 'Ligari'. I think we have them in England. We call them Butterfly Shrubs - Buddlea."

Not being one of the world's most enthusiastic of gardeners, my interest in this vital piece of botanical information waned somewhat as we approached the house. Alarmingly, voices could be heard, carried towards us on the evening breeze.

Stealing up to what was going to be the front door, we could hear whisperings and grunts coming from the bathroom. Surely someone couldn't be using it? There wasn't even a hole in the floor. The straining became even more intense. Throwing caution to the wind, I threw open the bathroom door. In the light of a kerosene lamp were two men crouched on the floor. One had a monkey wrench in his hand; the other had a spanner. Thank God. They were plumbers. The loo would soon be in business!

The following day we went shopping for household utensils and drove up to the house at the end of the afternoon. If we hadn't believed in fairies we did now.

The bathroom was finished, the kitchen units were in and the whole of the house interior had been painted. Only two things needed to be completed. The front door leant against the opening - it needed to be hung - and glass was required in the new bedroom window. Minor problems to say the least.

We jumped into the car and drove up to the Kafenio, for a celebratory drink.

The Kafenio only had a very limited choice of drinks - ouzo, metaxa, the local wine, soft drinks and beer. We ordered a, lemonade, a beer and two glasses - no straws - and poured ourselves shandies. Roxannie threw her up her hands and peals of laughter rang out as she pointed to our drinks and giggled, "cocktails." To Kafenio eenai mia Cocktail Bar!" She wouldn't join us for a shandy, but opened a bottle of orangeade instead. We toasted each other.

"See yia," said Roxannie, holding her glass high.

"Cheers," we said in English.

"Cheese," questioned Roxannie, "Pos eenai cheese?"

At this we all laughed. "Feta is a cheese," I said in greek. From then on Roxannie always toasted us in English - "feta."

We sipped our shandies slowly, drinking in the lovely view over the tiled rooftops, with the mountains and sea in the distance. The sun was warm and we stayed chatting to Roxannie in a combination of mime and stumbling Greek. We surprised ourselves how easily we could communicate - even though the village dialect was different to the pronunciations we had learned at College. In Crete the normal hard sounding Greek 'K' is pronounced as a soft 'ch'. This took some getting used to. Instead of 'supermarket' the Cretan pronunciation is 'supermarchet'.

Roxannie had been born in Afrata and was one of eight daughters and a brother. One sister had died, three now lived in Athens and the other three, including her ninety year old Mother, lived in Chicago. Dimitrios, whose daughter's house we had bought, was Roxannie's brother. He lived in Athens during the Winter and the Summer in Afrata.

In the fifties many people emigrated from Greece to seek their fortune. It was then that Roxannie's parents and sisters had decided to leave for America. With two small children and one on the way, she and Alekos stayed behind to take over the Kafenio, the sheep and goats, the olive groves and a small holding in Kolimbari. Times were hard. There was no road down the mountain, only a winding track, just wide enough to take a donkey. Every day Alekos had to make his way down to water all the tomatoes and cucumbers, as well as bring back essential supplies.

With Afrata being almost cut off as far as emergencies were concerned, the villagers lived an independant life. It was only in the sixties that a road was built and the village was connected to electricity and mains water. Why, even now Roxannie still relies heavily upon herbal medicine. This stemmed from childhood days, when it was difficult for a Doctor to reach Afrata. Roxannie was taught by her Mother and shown all the herbs that grew naturally around the mountainside and the powers they possessed for healing.

While times have changed, the close camerarderie of the village people remains, bonding them to the old country way of life, that was a haven for us.

Finishing our 'cocktail', we wished Roxannie goodbye and drove back to the Pension, looking forward to the big move tomorrow.

CHAPTER 5

Making the move to Afrata

We checked outof the Pension and with car piled high with all our luggage and essentials, we set forth to Afrata.

We had arranged with Mary to have a fridge-freezer delivered by twelve, but we still had plenty of time to stop at a large furniture store on the way. The factory and showroom was almost as large as the village it was set in. A huge variety of styles were displayed, from ornate suites with decorative wooden carvings and tapestry upholstery, to simple pine village furniture. The owner of this establishment sat at the back of the huge showroom, behind a huge desk. Unlike the typical salesman in England, dressed in a tie and suit, he was unshaven and sat there in his vest and braces. From his size, we judged him as a man who evidently enjoyed his food, for with considerable grunting and wheezing, he extricated himself from the chair and stood to welcome us, a little unsure of why tourists were here to buy his furniture.

Hearing we were speaking English, a broad smile spread across his face and he turned and shouted for his daughter to come inside to be an interpreter. When we addressed him in Greek, the grin spread even wider and he called out again. This time to his wife, with an instruction to bring coffee out to his English friends. We declined the kind offer and explained that we were moving to Afrata now, and need an immediate delivery. We were English AND buying a house in Crete? We could do no wrong.

Proudly the owner showed us round and agreed that our selection of pine village furniture was an excellent choice. He had chosen the wood himself and the items had been traditionally crafted by his sons, who worked in the factory. Walking round the displays, we selected a double bed with two bedside units, together with two single beds and a chest of drawers - all in pine which he had personally selected.

Recognising there would probably be many friends who would descend on us, we also bought a settee and an armchair, which both converted into put-you-up beds.

"Very useful. Very good design. Very hard wearing material. It will last very long time," gushed our super salesman.

There was eating to consider too. As most of the time this would be outdoors, we plumped for a large plastic table and six upholstered chairs.

Our shopping list now complete, it was time for negotiating the price. All the furniture was solidly built and at home would have cost two to three thousand pounds. With an element of friendly discussion and a hint of bargaining I was able to negotiate a buying price equivalent to one third of what it would have been in England. On shaking hands to cement the deal, I noticed Pauline had crept off and was trying hard to feign interest in a hideous floral settee.

Time was marching on. The furniture would be following us up the mountain within the next half hour and we had to stop at the Post Office in Kolimbari to top up our money reserves.

Squeezing ourselves into the tiny Fiat Panda and arranging bags and boxes around Pauline, we set off for the ten minute drive to Kolimbari. Reaching the village, we parked outside the 'tackithromeo' and much to the locals amusement, proceeded to stack saucepans, a pile of bedding, assorted items of kitchenware and a huge dustbin on the pavement, before Pauline could finally be extricated from the car. You may well wonder why couldn't she remain there while I changed the money? Alas, it was she who had the original foresight to collect and sign the traveller's cheques! Thus it was her signature that was now required.

Luckily there were no queues and we entered the cool shade of the building where three clerks sat, their eyes just visible over the counter. We handed over a traveller's cheque and passport to one clerk, who perused the documents and then handed them back. He directed us to pass everything back to the colleague sitting next to him, which we did. This official slowly filled in a form and requested we sign the cheque. Leisurely he reached for a rubber stamp and then proceeded to lazily ink it from a pad. Checking there was sufficient, he drew the stamp two feet above the paperwork and, with an almighty thump, that made the counter shake, he made the official mark - three times. Everything was passed back yet again and we were directed to pass the cheque to the colleague sitting beside him. Confirming that day's rate, the money was slowly counted out and checked again before, finally, we were given our drachmas.

Outside, we repeated the ritual of unloading everything onto the pavement, enabling my wife to get into the car. Once seated I then proceeded to squeeze the whole lot back in again. This time however, it seemed as if Pauline had miraculously gained weight during our sojourn to the Post Office. There was absolutely no way the dustbin was going to fit back in. Time was running out. A solution was needed - and fast.

Pleased with myself and with Pauline's head lovingly laid on my shoulder, we drove on through Kolimbari towards the monastery. With the road narrowing and several tourists waiting patiently to go in to the ancient building, I had to concentrate on my steering as the dustbin was jammed through the passenger window and was sticking out by half a metre. It could be a danger unless I gave everyone a wide berth. A friendly German gave the dustbin a friendly slap as we went by.

A voice whispered not so lovingly in my ear, "Move over. The rim of the dustbin is cutting into my neck."

As the car groaned up the mountain, in sympathy with Pauline, I could see below, and rapidly gaining on us, a large red and yellow van, with super salesman shoe horned behind the wheel. Beside him sat a rather large lady, while sandwiched between her and the door were two thin youths. By the time we reached the house, the van was right behind us. The convoy ground to a halt, behind another van and two pick-ups - one with our new fridge in the back.

In the house was the plumber, checking his handiwork in daylight. He was about to leave, but was going nowhere as the track outside was now blocked.

Nikos, the painter, was from the village. He was just putting the final touches to the outside. Not for him a prissy paint brush. Nikos liked to use something with a bit of covering power - a floor mop. The paint too was not your ordinary exterior emulsion. In typical village tradition he mixed his own paint from a heady concoction of lime, cement and water for a super brilliant white. Unfortunately, as we discovered later, it tended to wash off during the winter rains!

Quietly crocheting beneath the shade of the old olive tree, sat his wife, Argirula, taking in all the hustle and bustle up and down the garden path.

With lots of wheezing and coughing, the furniture was ferried into the house. Super salesman had brought his wife to look round and see just how the English live. At arm's length, like a butler serving tea and cucumber sandwiches, he carried a single plastic chair and reverently placed it on the verandha. This was not for his wife. It was where he could sit down and direct proceedings, by barking instructions to his two helpers, while draping himself over the blue railings.

Inside was chaos, with pieces of double bed all over the floor. The two youths painstakingly examined each piece before attempting its assembly. In the midst of all this, the two wives stood and examined our sofa bed, admiring how practical it was with all the storage space beneath.

Their discussion was interrupted by the unveiling of the 'fridge. To "oohs," and "ahhs," the outer carton was torn away to reveal ... nothing more than a 'fridge.

However, this did not prevent the plumber, Nikos, Argirula, super salesman, his wife, the two youths and Uncle Tom Cobbly, this was something to inspect and marvel over. There was no doubt, this was an excellent purchase. Such storage space and the oh so handy size of the freezer section. Yes. We certainly had their approval.

Returning to the assembly line, the two youths gave a final "bravo." The bed was now completed - a two hundred weight masterpiece in solid pine. Unfortunately it would have been a far better idea to have assembled it in suite. The next five minutes were spent in trying to squeeze the bed through the door into the bedroom. Suffice to say the head and foot boards had to first be removed before the base could be cadjoled past the door jamb and into its rightful position.

Eventually the fridge and all the furniture were put in their rightful places and the delivery men were gone. Silver haired Nikos and Argirula bade us farewell, but not without making sure we would call on them for coffee during the next few days, once we were settled.

There was one last problem, however. The front door was fast disappearing down the path on the plumber's back.

"Ela 'tho," I shouted.

The stooping figure stopped and a voice beneath the door expalined what the problem was. When originally he had measured the opening, the metal door had fitted perfectly. Now, due to the tiles having been laid, there was a little problem - it didn't fit, but there was nothing to worry about. He was an expert at cutting doors. He would be back.

"When," I shouted?

The door shrugged. "No problem. Soon."

Well. At last we were here and everything looked just as we had imagined it would. The lounge was painted white and on the floor, stone coloured tiles had been laid. The kitchen area had been fitted with units in the palest of blue and the new furniture blended perfectly to create an effect which was light and fresh. Without the front door, perhaps a little more fresher than one would have wished.

By the time night fell, we had unpacked and stored everything away. In addition we had hung pictures, curtains and a toilet roll holder; not to mention rewiring plugs on the cooker, hair dryer, kettle, table lamps and hi fi. Too tired to go out for a meal, we made do with biscuits and coffee and relaxed on the verandha, sitting in the warm night air, watching the stars and planning what should be done to the garden. It was ten o'clock and tomorrow we had a busy day ahead of us. Pauline decided to have a shower and I sat there immersing myself in the perfect silence - with just the murmur of voices way up in the village above me. This house in Afrata was hardly a luxury villa, but its position and the villager's warm, open, friendliness made it a place that was something special.

A scream brought me back to reality. It was Pauline. I ran into the bathroom. The shower curtains were drawn and I could hear the sound of water spraying against the blue plastic. Another scream rang out. Like a scene from Psycho, I fearfully drew back the curtain.

"I keep getting an elctric shock. The bloody plumber's not wired the water heater properly!"

She was right. When you had wet hands, you received a shock whenever the taps were touched. Asking at the village, later, everyone laughed. It appeared they all used the same plumber and they had all got used to having little electric shocks - no problem.

We were English - it was a problem.

Failing to find a bare wire, or any obvious fault, we came up with the ultimate solution. Now, we have in our shower, shampoo, sponge, soap and ... a rubber glove for turning the tap off. No home in Afrata should be without one.

The following day we awoke to sun streaming through the bedroom windows. There was nothing to stop it - not a single pane of glass to be seen. Besides having a sadistic delight in electrocuting his customers, the plumber was apparently also a craftsman in metalwork. He had made both the front door and the window frames for our new bedroom.

Unfortunately he was not a glazier - hence the draught.

Bathing in the sunlight, I suddenly became aware of a quiet rustling sound, outside in the kitchen. I nudged Pauline. We both lay there listening. There it was again. Slowly - and very bravely I thought, I slid open the bedroom door.

All was quiet.

I tip-toed over towards the sink. There it was again. I bent down, my face close to the cupboard door, beads of perspiration forming on my face. I felt cold and a little exposed with no clothes on and an opening behind me, where the front door should have been. There it was again - that rustling sound. God. It couldn't be. Summoning every ounce of nerve, my fingers slowly grasped the cupboard door. I knew what was behind there. An hypnotic fear numbed my brain. I held my breath. With a cry I threw open the door. A mouse. A mouse. "Ahhhhh." I ran towards the haven of the bedroom and the huge mouse - all of three inches long - ran behind the cupboard.

While Pauline laughed, I concentrated on a master plan to rid us of this plague.

The mouse had obviously found something to its liking in the waste bin. I went to the 'fridge and cut a small square of feta cheese - it was a Greek mouse - and placed it on top of the rubbish. Taking a pencil, I delicately stood it vertically, bringing the lid down to counter balance the trap. Simple, yet ingenious. In its haste for the tasty titbit, the mouse would nudge the pencil, the lid would come down, and it would be imprisoned, inside the waste bin.

With the trap set, I gently closed the cupboard door and sat down to wait. The minutes ticked by and then I heard it - a scuffling, a rustling and a loud plop as the lid closed, like a door slamming shut on a prison cell.

"Geronimo!" It had worked. Ah. Now there was a problem. I had to remove the mouse from the house. Pulling my dressing gown tightly around me, I bravely opened the cupboard door. Steeling myself to reach for the bin, I suddenly wondered whether it could get out from the bottom. Ahhhh. There was a rustle from inside and I jumped back.

"What are you, a man or a mouse," mused Pauline, behind me, thoroughly enjoying the spectacle.

Goaded into action, I closed my eyes, grasped the bin with both hands and lifted. As the rustling inside became more frantic, my feet moved faster. Speeding across the lounge I leapt onto the verandha, my dressing gown swirling behind me in the slip stream as I flew down the garden path. Reaching the end, I threw the bin to the left, in a style that would have drawn roars of appreciation at Twickenham. I veered to the right to get as far away as possible.

Grasping the opportunity to escape, the beast galloped away into the hedgerow. It was the law of the jungle. Man, the mighty hunter, once again reigned supreme. Like a triumphant Theseus returning from having vanquished the Minotaur, I proudly returned to the house for a well earned cup of tea.

Having recovered from the scars of battle, it was now time for a different challenge - how to solve the draught in our bedroom.

Our friendly plumber was very proud of the bedroom windows he had made. As he pointed out, they were of excellent quality and extremely strong, yet he had still managed to make the frames very narrow. Not listing glazing among his many talents, he had suggested we unscrew each window and transport the four frames to Tavronitis, the village some ten kilometres from Afrata. There was a glazier there who would work very quickly. So, following instructions, we loaded the frames into the car and I set off down the mountain.

Upon my arrival, the glazier's wife explained that her husband was very busy, but he would be pleased to cut and fit the glass the very next day. That wasn't so much of a problem. We didn't have a door, so what did it matter if we didn't have windows either? Being assured the frames would be ready at six o'clock the following evening, I thanked her and set off back to Afrata.

Meanwhile, back at the house there was a coffee morning going on. While Pauline was doing some housework, through the open door she became aware of three faces looking at her through the verandha railings. It was three women from the village who had come to introduce themselves. In England, if you are lucky, a neighbour will bring out a tray of tea and biscuits to welcome new arrivals. In Afrata it is a sprig of fresh herbs and a huge fish.

While Pauline made iced coffee for everyone, three ladies from the village, Sophia, Anna and Eleni, proceeded to take the huge fish out of a plastic bag. It must have weighed about two kilos and had been caught that very morning by one of the husbands who had a tiny boat down in the cove. Laying the fish on its side on top of our newly painted white garden wall, Sophia expertly scraped the fish with a fierce looking knife. The shimmering scales resembled tiny pieces of plastic and were obviously far too tough to eat. Once this job had been completed to everyone's satisfaction, the fins were removed and the fish was all cleaned out ready for barbecueing that evening.

As I arrived back, the coffee morning was just coming to an end, with the women waving their goodbyes, each treasuring a rose, which Pauline had picked from our garden - a small token of our thanks for their friendship and making us feel so welcome.

As we had already discovered, the act of giving was considered to be of far greater importance than the gift itself.

CHAPTER 6

Alekos and Roxannie

Under a clear blue sky, with the incessant burr of cicadas filling the air, we sat outside the Kafenio with Roxannie, sipping a cool lemonade. Everywhere was still. Four hundred metres above, the mountains towered over the sleepy village. Beneath us pantiled roofs of white and ochre painted houses, framed a picture of olive groves leading into the gorge and beyond, the sea.

As we sat there, drinking in this magnificent scene, deep within the darkness of the Kafenio the squeak of an opening door, and a shuffling and snorting could be heard. Alekos had awoken from his afternoon nap.

After a brief splashing of water, the dignified figure emerged into the sunlight. "Kako pethee," he smiled and the palm of his hand chopped the air in the traditional symbol of scolding. Although I am a Grandfather, his twenty five years seniority allowed him to call me, "naughty boy," by way of a greeting. The 'naughty' part referred to the standing joke between us that, as old men, we were entitled to ogle the female tourists that sped by the Kafenio, in minimum attire, glued to the pillion of their mopeds.

As Alekos walked towards us, I couldn't resist a grin. He had forgotten to do up the fly buttons on his trousers.

Now it was my turn. "Kako pethee." Laughing, I pointed.

He looked down, shrugged his shoulders and spread his hands in a gesture of sublime resignation. Smiling, he explained there was no problem. The 'pouli' - bird - in his trousers was fast asleep. There would only be a problem if a tourist were to happen past and wake it up. With a cackle, he ducked as Roxannie aimed a clip to the back of his head. Amidst much laughter, he made himself respectable, pulled up a well worn chair with its raffia seat and sat down with us to talk.

Alekos' surname was Papatherakis. The last four letters - 'akis' - always signified a true Cretan name. However, there was more to Alekos' name. His family had always lived in Afrata and indeed, his own great-great grandfather had been the village priest. In the Greek Orthodox religion, priests are allowed to marry, although only single priests are invariably considered for higher positions. I calculated that Alekos' forefather must have been born in the early part of the nineteenth century. At that time Crete was still under the domination of eight hundred years of Turkish occupation. During this terrible time, their language and culture was totally suppressed as the foreign power exercised total dominance over the Cretans.

In Afrata there lived a Turk who ruled the local community with a rod of iron. He viewed the villagers with contempt, and demonstrated his total power, by demanding sexual rights over any local girl of his choice. Finally the true Cretan character came to the fore at this affront to the villagers' honour. When plea after plea was ignored there was only one option left open. For the first time in his life, Alekos' great-great-grandfather became a thief and stole a gun. Creeping into the Turk's house, the Papas avenged his community and simply shot the tyrant dead. The inevitable consequence wrought havoc, as the area was beseiged by Turkish forces looking for the murderer. By this time however, the local hero had been spirited away into the mountains. These huge rocky outposts had served the Cretans well, for only they knew the hidden gullies and caves which were inaccessible to everyone but themselves. It was here that the Papas and his family lived, safe from the inevitable penalty of death.

For more than thirty years the family lived in mountains away from the eyes of the Turks, helped by their friends in Afrata who smuggled them necessary supplies under protection of darkness. In recognition of his action, the family became known as Papatherakis, in honour of the brave Papas.

With so much talking, Alekos was now in need of a coffee and disappeared into the Kafenio. A few moments later he reappeared, carrying a tray, on which was balanced two glasses of water, a Greek coffee, a saucer of peanuts and two glasses of tskouthia. Roxannie was given water and Pauline and I were given the local spirit. Sounding like a Glaswegian threat - "see yia" - we clinked glasses and cups in the traditional Greek toast.

As always, when served alcohol, a small snack is offered, hence the peanuts. A nut cracker being out of the question, I followed Alekos' intruction, took a nut, and, placing it on the corner of the table, aimed a fist at the salted shell. The blow demolished the nut into miniscule fragments, leaving us to separate bits of shell to find the tiny pieces of peanut. From this poor first attempt, I can now claim to be expert in nut cracking. One slam and the shell cracks, as sweet as a nut, leaving two perfectly formed peanuts as nibbles with our drinks.

Relaxing over our drinks, I asked Roxannie about her life in Afrata.

Roxannie's family had also lived in the village for many generations. She pointed to a derelict stone house below us. There was now only two walls standing. She could remember her grandfather living there. He was a Captain in the merchant navy and was very rich. She knew this, because as a litle girl, playing by the house with her sisters, he arrived home from sea.

Seeing the children, he reached into his pocket, pulled out some golden coins and threw a shower into the air. Shrieking, the girls ran hither and thither to catch them as they chinked and clinked over the stone path. However, one day, he went away and she never saw him again. Now a grandmother, Roxannie looks back to that time all those years ago and shrugs her shoulders. With a smile she says, "it's like the money. We never saw that again either."

We sat and listened to Roxannie as she told us of the time she was a girl in Afrata.

The village then, some fifty years or more ago, was a little community almost cut off by the mountains surrounding it. Access was by coat from the little cove, or by donkey along a tiny track worn along the side of the mountain down to the next village of Kolimbari far below.

There were nine in Roxannie's family, her mother and father, a brother and six sisters. There was not much money to be had, yet life was good. They had plenty of food, their own wine, the closeness of friends and relatives around them and, of course, the magnificent natural surroundings. They all worked hard, governed by the seasons. January for picking the olives and citrus fruits, September for the grapes and making wine, while the sheep, goats and vegetables demanded constant attention of food and water the whole year round.

This idyll was shattered in 1941 by war.

The main thrust of the German advance into Crete came at Malame. This tiny airstrip, still there today, is only twelve kilomtres away from Afrata, across the bay. It was Malame that saw the largest air assault ever launched. On May 20th, thousands of men parachuted into the area. The air was filled with planes dropping their troops in thousands. Below stood villagers, including many women, armed with knives and farm implements, ready to defend their country against all odds. They waited, ready to kill their attackers directly they landed, as they struggled, helplessly, to free themselves from their parachute harnesses.

The village was attacked by troops landing in the tiny cove. Fighting was firece as the English and Greeks fought in vain to prevent the Germans from landing, but to no avail. The allies retreated back through the mountains, leaving the villagers to suffer the consequences. For several days bloated bodies lay on the beach, or were smashed against the rocks, before they were given a burial.

Afrata was desparately poor, but proud, refusing to help the invading troops, yet despite everything, their courage knew no bounds. They would protect any allied soldier from falling into the hands of the Reich - even though this was extremely dangerous if they were ever discovered. For every allied soldier who was sheltered, the Germans would shoot ten Greeks. Many villagers were shot and executed at Kolimbari.

A Lieutenant, leading the German soldiers who patrolled Afrata, was ever fearful of the courageous Cretans. So much so that one day he pulled little Roxannie out from the crowd of villagers rounded up in the square. He then forced the frightened nine year old to taste the water his troops were about to drink, frightened that it might be poisoned.

Food for the villagers was scarce. Roxannie's father managed to push his boat out to sea, without being seen and caught several fish. Thankful that his family would at last have sustenance for a few days, his thanks were short lived. As their mother was cooking this unexpected luxury, troops burst in and took the only meal the family had had for eight days. They were virtually existing on a diet of horta - weeds collected from the mountainside, boiled and served in olive oil.

Three allied airmen had been shot down and parachuted into the surrounding mountains. Two were from New Zealand, the other from England. Ignoring the terrible punishment if caught, Alekos and our painter, Nikos, who was only a boy, sheltered the airmen in a cave above the village. Every night for three months they took the fugitives food and water, before the resistance could arrange to get the allies away to the South of Crete and eventual freedom.

The German occupation lasted for four long years.

When Roxannie was fifteen, she fell in love. Finding any excuse, she would hide behind the olive trees to look at Alekos tending his sheep and goats. Ten years older than Roxannie, Alekos was a typical mountain villager, proud and strong, with tremendous stamina that allowed him to walk the rocky terrain as sure footed as his goats. Traditionally village men married late, generally to girls several years younger than themselves.

Alekos maintains this age difference is important, because as you get older you need a good strong woman to look after you and your animals!

Alekos pretended not to see his ardent admirer, smiling to himself whenever he suddenly turned and caught a glimpse of this raven haired girl. Roxannie would feast her eyes on Alekos as he worked, fearing he would turn and see her. If he looked round she would dart back behind a tree, her heart pounding. After a moment or two she would venture another peep. So the game went on, but over the days and weeks, from shy smiles and exchanging a few words, a romance began to blossom.

After several weeks Roxannie confided in Stella, her eldest sister and showed her the letters from Alekos, which she kept hidden in her bra. Alarmed at the consequences of her being alone, without a chaperone, Stella informed her father.

Weighing some two hundred and ten kilos and standing two metres high, her father was a giant of a man - a figure to be feared and obeyed without question. With moustache bristling with rage, he stormed into the Kafenio and in front of the whole family, literally threw Roxannie across the room in a furious rage. His fury was uncontrollable.

"Had she no shame? Did she not consider the disgrace her family would have to suffer? Did she not care his reputation would be shot to pieces?"

That was exactly the fate he intended for Papatherakis. With two belts of ammunition slung over his chest, he reached for his gun. Ignoring the sobbing pleas from Roxannie, he threw open the door and was gone. His honour was at stake. Ammends would have to be made.

At this point in the story, proceedings were interupted by the pop pop pop of a moped and round the corner chugged two tourists. As always Alekos went to great pains to offer a friendly welcome and set the pair down at a table. With their sensible hats, and the man wearing socks with his sandals, they were obviously English. From their pallor, it was obvious this was only the second or third day of their holiday. Failing to understand Alekos' attentive welcome in Greek, the woman, speaking very loudly and very slowly, ordered "two teas please."

We smiled to ourselves as Alekos called across to Roxannie, "thio tsye."

Several minutes later Alekos strode purposefully out of the Kafenio, carrying a tray with two glasses of a steaming, pale yellow liquid. With much aplomb and a flourish, he served the surprised tourists with their order, ignoring their plaintiff pleas of "... but we ordered tea." Having duly completed his job as waiter, he returned to the Kafenio for his walking stick and Bart Simpson baseball cap. He had other chores to attend to, and set off for the twenty minute walk up the mountain to where his sheep were penned.

Meanwhile the two English holidaymakers were wondering what on earth had been served to them. Leaning forward, they wrinkled their noses at the smell emnating from the glasses. Unable to contain ourselves anymore, we burst into laughter, but taking pity on their plight, I called out, in perfect English, "Do you need any help? Would you like milk and sugar with your tea?"

As all foreigners are obviously deaf, the woman, who was obviously the appointed linguist spoke in loud dulcit tones, "we order-ed tea. I bel-ieve the wait-er und-er-stood what I asked for. This must be for some-one else. Is it for you," and she repeated the sentence in mime.

Perplexed by my laughing, she tried to placate me by enquiring, "my, you do speak excel-lent Eng-lish. Have you ever trav-elled to the UK?"

By this time our sides were aching. "I'm so sorry," I spluttered, "I am as English as you are. I know you ordered tea and that is what was served. I am afraid Roxannie has never heard of Earl Grey. What you have there is mountain tea. It is a mixture of herbs collected from the mountainside, infused as a tea. The villagers swear by it as a cure for indigestion and stomach ailments, but I must admit it is an aquired taste. Perhaps you would be better off with an ice cold frappe of coffee? It's far more thirst quenching on a day like this."

"But we always have tea in the afternoon. If you don't have proper English tea, as we're used to, then I am afraid we shall have to go elsewhere," and with nose in air, she flounced off towards the moped, with her husband shuffling along behind. With a pop pop pop and a puff of blue smoke they were gone.

Emerging from the Kafenio with a plate of figs as a gift for the two tourists, Roxannie shrugged her shoulders, smiled and the three of us sat down to each peel ourselves some of the delicious fruit, which had just been freshly picked.

"So what happened next, when your father threatened to kill Alekos," I asked, remembering the tale that was so rudely interrupted?

Running through the village, his mountain boots thudding along the stony track, his face set in a blaze of fury, Roxannie's father had only one thought in his raging mind. To kill Alekos. He stopped by the last house, with olive groves below, and the gorge in front of him. With gun held high above his head, he shouted, "Papatherakis, ela na se tho - Papatherakis, come let me see you," and his voice boomed down the gorge, richoqueting from rock to rock, building into a crescendo of echoes. Again he shouted, but when silence reigned, just the faint tinkling of bells could be heard from the goats on the craggs high above. The huge man scrambled down the slope into the olive groves, determined in his quest to avenge the family's honour. Reaching the steps leading to the tiny chapel in the rock, he stopped. His eyes ran along the cliffs of the gorge seeking his prey, his senses acutely tuned to the terrain.

"So you want to see me? Well here I am."

The big man spun round with a snarl, his gun held before him, pointed at Alekos' heart.

The young man held his arms wide in submission, in one hand a cloth, wrapped around some goat's cheese and a loaf of bread. In the other was a flask of tskouthia.

"Do you have time for a bite to eat, before you toast my death?"

Suffice to say, Alekos survived and he and Roxannie were married in the village church in 1947.

Within a year Costas, a son was born, followed by a daughter, Myropi and two further boys, Michylie and Andonis.

Most of Roxannie's family left to start a new life in Athens and America, but Alekos and Roxannie preferred to remain in Afrata. They took over the Kafenio, the small holding and the olive groves and, together, built a life for themselves. A life which was hard, but one shared equally. Their love for each other and the true values of life they have learned are treasures to be envied.

CHAPTER 7

An English Country Garden

Having had all the building work completed and bought all the furniture, we had, at last, the makings of a home.

Sitting on the verandha, sipping a beer beneath the spread of the old olive tree, we began to plan the next project - an English country garden. Our land was broken into two parts. Behind and to the side of the house, separated by a low wall, were olive trees and citrus fruit, growing out of a metre high carpet of yellowed, dried out weeds. For the time being we felt this could remain 'au naturel'.

From where we sat, there was an area eighteen metres wide by thirty metres at the longest point. To the locals this was prime agricultural land ideal for melons, tomatoes, cucumbers and grapes. Flowers? They grew in pots. Why on earth waste rich soil on something that wasn't edible? Even a garden full of weeds was more useful - it could be used to feed the sheep, but flowers? Bah!

With beds here, paths there, annuals, perrenials, seeds, bulbs, shrubs and trees, the garden was taking shape in our minds.

Now for the hard bit. Theory was all very well, but putting it into practice was altogether a site more strenuous!

The first thing we had to do was build an irrigation system and the place to go for that was the local farmer's shop, down in

Kolimbari. This mecca of all things agricultural was a cross between a Victorian emporium and a car boot sale. Entering the shop invariably meant there was only sufficient space for three or four customers, because of all the boxes, cartons and stacks of equipment piled everywhere. It was like an Aladdin's cave. Hoes, forks, spades, all with long, immensely thick wooden handles, which could only have been wielded by Hercules - surely, never by mere mortals? There were plumbing, carpentry and building tools of every type, huge portable tanks in plastic, brass and copper, which you filled with chemicals for spraying, generators, rotovators - the list was endless. Every conceivable product you could ever think of, connected with agriculture.

Several customers waited impatiently to be served, while others, even more impatient, had gone behind the counter to give their intended purchases a closer inspection. Meanwhile, others, also behind the counter, who may well have been sales staff, chatted with a few friends who had dropped in to share a snack. During all this time, the cashier kept up an endless banter with anyone who would listen.

Having been brought up in England and indoctrinated to wait my turn in an orderly queue, this maxim just did not apply here. I could be doomed to a lifetime of waiting, or refute this ingrained doctrine and push and shove like the rest of the locals. However, there was one small problem. Who the hell was serving? I tapped on the shoulder of one man standing behind the counter with his back to me.

"Signomi," I ventured?

He turned, looked at me, looked at his shoulder as if it had been tainted with something nasty and then walked away. Meanwhile, two more people squeezed in. The tidal wave of straining flesh this created, swept me to the priphery of the crowd and I found myself wedged, half sat upon a pile of cartons, with a chain saw poking out from between my legs. As I struggled to retain a proper standing position, so a satisfied customer, clutching his bag of purchases, fought his way out. Taking advantage of the space this created, I found myself back in the middle of the crowd, determined this time to hold my place. It was still almost impossible to detect who was serving, as several, obviously old hands, just helped themselves from the shelves, or from the dozens of bins which contained all sorts of plastic and metal components. Finally, I was pretty sure I had identified an assistant. The fact he was lounged over the counter, chatting for what seemed an age, to a life long chum, was neither here nor there. Gradually I edged closer. Then, in all the hub hub, I squeezed into pole position - ready to jump in as soon as the assistant stopped talking. They stopped. I opened my mouth and a great booming voice drowned my rather timid attempt to attract attention. As the voice belonged to a rather large man with a week's stubble, wearing a combat jacket and a gun slung casually over his shoulder, I rationalised it was probably alright if he went first.

This was ridiculous. As someone who prides himself on having restaurant presence, my inability to get served was becoming a dent to my ego. As people came and went, as jostles were returned with shoves, as orders were shouted and wild gesticulations waved over my head, those immortal words came to mind - "I can't stands no more." Like Popeye swallowing a mouthful of spinach, I shed nealy fifty years of English convention and, at the top of my voice, shouted at a sales assistant idly chatting, "Ela na sou po." The effect was electric. There was a total stunned silence, followed by laughter, much back slapping and grins, but it worked. A tourist speaking Greek - whatever next?

I believe it is the way I spoke which created such an effect. I like to think my accent is as attractive to the Greek ear as Sacha Distel's French accent is to the English. Unfortunately, while Sacha Distel may be able to stun a roomful of ladies with his accent, I can only claim to have silenced a dozen beefy farmers.

"Ne? Ti theleis," asked the assistant? I was home and dry - or almost.

"Why does a tourist ask for a hundred metres of hosepipe? Do you not have this in London? Ah. you have a house here and it is for the garden? You grow flowers? Here in Crete we use our land for food to help keep our bellies full. Flowers? What use are they? Tell your wife to grow her flowers in pots."

Very begrudgingly I came away with the hose and a large bagful of plastic joints and taca - tacas. I still don't know what these are called, but Michylie, Alekos' son had told us we needed these tiny sprays which screwed into the hose by each plant and went tac, tac, tac, as they drip, drip, drip water onto the ground. In the event our water pressure was far too high and instead of tac, tac sounds, it went taca, taca and the name stuck.

Gradually we planted the garden, forever extending the irrigation system by joining on new spurs to reach this new stub or that new plant. First thing in the morning I would turn on the water and like a great steam locomotive the flow would reach each taca- taca, hissing and beltching, before gurgling onto the next. Up and down the garden it spluttered, to finish on a huge terra cotta urn, which houses the bourgainvillea, designed to grow along the verandha.

Unfortunately, there is more to landscaping than just the

planting, as I was about to discover. I woke up one morning to be told that today was the day we would be collecting stones. Not your common or garden little jobs, but damn great big ones. We were talking hernia material! Why? Because we needed to build some pathways in the garden.

"Why not ask Michylie to lay some cement," I protested lamely?

No. We were going out and about looking for great flat lumps of rock. It didn't seem to matter that a wheelbarrow wasn't in our inventory of tools and equipment.

For three days I laboured, like an inmate at Alcatraz, as I lifted stones heavy enough to impress Olympic Selectors seeking weight-lifting contenders. Finding a suitable piece of potential pathway, I would snatch lift it to my stomach and, bent double, wobble back to the cache I had built in the garden, like some demented squirrel. With the hot sun baking down, I stumbled back over the inhospitable terrain, time and time again, while through sweat filled eyes it seemed the garden was moving further and further away. Still I laboured, scouring the ground for broken bits of mountain. Perfect specimens of half buried rock proved to be nothing more than mere tips the iceberg. Finally, a broken man, I had to report there was no more. The supply of rock near to the house had been exhausted.

My taskmaster was not impressed. Ordered to the car, we drove to other sites, where likely looking candidates were wrested from where they had lain for millenia and unceremoniously dumped into the boot. Finally we worked our way down to the beach.

"This one?"

"No. It's not flat enough."

"This one?"

"No. It's the wrong colour."

"This one?"

"No. It's too small."

With boot laden to the gunwales, the car wheelied its way back to the house.

Eventually my slave driver passed all the materials as being of satisfactory standard and proclaimed that building could commence. Taking my Greek hoe, an implement that must surely have been used unchanged for thousands of years, I marked out pathways to be built. Tirelessly I worked from sunrise to sunset, beneath an unrelenting sun which bore down on my poor, wracked and torn body, squeezing out every little drop of moisture - but still I toiled. Each rock had to have its own bed of pebbles to lie on, before being tapped down to the level of its neighbour. Like a giant jig saw, each piece fitted together and gradually the paths grew. One to the shower behind the olive tree, another to the yet to be built barbecue and still another leading right across the garden to link with the jungle at the back of the house. I now know what it must have been like building the great Palace at Knossos.

Alekos and his son, Michylie, always passed the time of day with us. Both would stop and comment as the garden began to take shape.

Alekos brought the sheep down to the pen near our house in

the early evening, where the flock spent the night - we were never up at five thirty in the morning when he took them back up the mountain!

You could set your watch by Michylie's truck coming down the track at six thirty in the evening to water the goats and sheep. Unlike his brothers and sister, Michylie had decided to stay in the village and derived an income from farming and building work. He was tall, lean and muscular, with wavy brown hair and sported a luxuriant Cretan style moustache. He had a fine sense of humour as was proved on one particular evening.

A toot toot heralded the arrival of Michylie's truck. He was early. It was only six and what's more he had stopped by the gate. Alekos and his son got out looking very pleased with themselves. Michylie was grinning, his white teeth just visible beneath the moustache.

"Yassas. We have a gift for you and Paulina. It will help your garden to grow," and they both dissolved into helpless fits of laughter.

I walked round to the back of the truck and realised what they were laughing at. There, stood an assorted range of plastic and paper sacks, each one filled to the brim and overflowing with sheep's droppings!

"Michylie and I shovelled this for you as a gift. It does not smell - see," and Alekos plunged his hand into the nearest sack pulling out a great fistful to show me.

"I believe you, I believe you," I uttered beseechingly, but knew it was to no avail.

Like some awful innitiation ceremony, I had to go through the ordained ritual, or our friends would be offended. Taking a deep breath, I thrust my hand into the sack, my fingers closed on the dried, dark brown beads and a fistful was pulled out into the clean mounatin air.

"Now smell. See. The dung, it does not smell. It is clean," laughed Michylie.

Gingerly, very gingerly, I proferred my nostrils like an antelope sniffing for a scent on the wind. Low and behold. It was true. I couldn't smell a thing.

"You must crumble it like this, into powder and place it around each plant. Water it into the soil and your plants will grow good and strong," and he demonstrated by taking a fistful and ground it between his palms. "It is the finest thing for your garden."

Thanking our friends for their thoughtful and generous gift, we waved them goodbye and got down to the daunting task of powdering eight bags. It was amazing stuff. Presumably several months old, it had been left to naturally dry out in the sun. There was really no smell at all.

Within an hour or so each plant and shrub had been administered a pick-me-up and wherever we looked, there were little dark brown fairy rings all around the garden. I turned on the water as per instructions.

In minutes the miracle fertiliser had reverted back to its natural state and the whole garden reeked of a farmyard. Even though it was still warm, we closed all the windows in the house, but we were too late. The pungent smell had already wafted inside. We were doomed. The heady aroma stayed with us through the night, silencing even the cicadas. It was fainter in the morning, thank heavens, but on opening the door to greet the morning, it was still there in the garden. Like some festering growth, it vanished under the hot, dry sun, only to return when feeding on the merest hint of moisture.

For three days and nights we suffered.

On the fourth day there was a marked improvement - or our nasal passages had by this time been traumatised. Amazingly, the hot sun, together with liberal watering and the magical manure had performed a miracle. What should have been a month's growth in England, had been achieved in a matter of days in this paradise.

Almost like a time lapse film, you could almost see everything growing. Like wildfire, the news that water was available quickly spread through the animal community. Birds of all sorts bathed and drunk in the pools of water surrounding the plants. What looked like a ferret would dart in and out of the garden, while some mysterious beast would visit at night and leave dozens of holes scooped out of the soil. Michylie told us this was an 'asvos' - badger and there were many in the countryside around. The damp soil in our garden encouraged worms, which provided a fast food restaurant for passing badgers. Unfortunately this did not do wonders for the plants, many of which were left with their roots exposed.

One night we were woken by a terrible noise. A chomping and a tearing and much snorting filled the quiet night air. Whatever it was sounded pretty damned big. I knew there were no large animals on Crete, so at worst it could only be a Cretan Fox - something like a ferocious Racoon.

Gingerly we slowly opened the front door. An almighty loud

squeak wrought the air as the hinges objected to being moved at this god forsaken hour. The sound did nothing to alarm the creature, for the nightmarish sounds continued. Pauline reached for the outside light and the garden was flooded with light. The noises stopped. In the shadows, where the beam fell short, stood a dark shape. The creature's head slowly turned towards us, as if to ask, "what's up can't you sleep?" It was Alekos' mule. It had been dining on the artichokes we had been carefully nurturing. Where the animal had squeezed into a position to give him access to the artichokes, his rear end hovered over the roses. What goes in, must come out. The animal was a perfect re-cycling machine. The sound of a four gun salute echoed round the mountainside and another measure of fertilizer was perfectly deposited on a welcoming plant.

When told his mule had slipped its tether during the night and had eaten all our artichokes, Alekos laughed. "Did he wake you with his music," he asked joyfully? "Rat-a-tat-tat, rat-a-tat-tat - just like Beethoven." Alekos obviously had a more musical ear than us. However, the roses did come on a treat and they did smell heavenly.

Every day an old woman shuffled slowly past the house as she made her way to the field where she grew tomatoes and cucumbers.

"Kali maaaaaaira," should would croak. This time however, she had with her a goat on a lead. Prancing along behind, like naughty children, were two delightful kids. They couldn't have been more than a month or two old and they chased each other up and down the stony track, looking for whatever mischief they could find next - and they found it in our garden. It was nine in the morning and we were busy brewing coffee and cutting some fruit ready for breakfast. Stepping outside, we saw the kids on the wall, standing on their hind legs, innocently chomping on all the nuts and leaves on our almond tree.

"Hey!"

The shout didn't stop them for a second, but picking a stone to throw at them did. Two minutes later they reappeared again to grab another mouthful of leaves, before a pebble, hitting the wall they were standing on, made them scamper off. You could almost imagine them giggling as they reappeared yet again, on discovering this enjoyable new game.

Maintaining the English national trait for being kind to animals, we lost half a tree to these urchins. The old lady returned from her work in the fields, leading the nanny goat and, like the Pied Piper, the kids scampered away to dance along behind.

"Kali maaaaaaira," she waved.

With the sun, our garden depended upon copious levels of water. One evening we suffered a cut. This was not unusual, but as there was still no water the following day, we were beginning to get a little concerned, not so much for the garden, but more so for our own needs. Without being able to wash, having to brush your teeth and using beer as a mouth sloosh, all left a lot to be desired.

At five in the afternnon, some twenty four hours later, I heard, "Ela, ela - na, na." It was Alekos calling his sheep out of the olive grove to follow him along the road.

"Yassou, kako pethie," he greeted me. On asking him when did he think the water would be turned on, he looked surprised. Telling me to wait for ten minutes, he led the flock down to their pen, before returning. Together we walked up towards the village to the house above ours - a distance of three hundred metres or so. Considering he was in his seventies, I was breathless as I struggled to keep level with him up the steep incline. On reaching the house, he strode purposefully through the garden calling, "Katerina, ela." Without waiting, he made his way to a large shrub and crawled under. I could see in the undergrowth, a black plastic water pipe, connected to a spur by a bright red lever. Turning it, Alekos emerged from the bushes, a triumphant expression on his face.

"Ekeis to nero, torra - you have water now."

I turned as a little old lady appeared. She was extremely nervous. Dressed completely in black, she wore thin metal glasses, a black kerchief over her grey hair and had a wonderful smile like a kindly, benevolent nun from The Sound of Music.

"Signomi, signomi," she apologised, her hands fluttering with embarassment.

Apparently, our water supply did not have its own meter. While we paid the bills submitted by the Water Company, this was always based upon a percentage of the metered reading. As we were using a lot of water for the garden, the pressure to Katerina's house was reduced and she often turned off our supply for a few minutes. This time, unfortunately, she had forgotten to turn it back on again. She couldn't aplogise enough. Because of the inconvenience to us both, we agreed it would be far more preferable if we were to have our own supply.

As Alekos had the only telephone in the village, he agreed to call the Water Company and a plumber and we would all meet at seven the following evening by the meter clocks.

The clocks were where the mains water supply was spurred into six small bore plastic pipes which ran down the mountain to each house. Before each pipe snaked away, it was connected to a small round meter, which was sealed and registered the volume of water used by each house.

As instructed, we assembled at the designated point, from where we could see our house way, way below. We now know that appointments here are rarely made for a precise time. Give or take an hour, either way, is perfectly acceptable. Fortunately, we only had to wait for thirty minutes before a veritable crowd arrived. In its midst Alekos could be seen - and heard. With much shoulder shrugging, clucking and a lot of head jerking - the traditional sign for'no', it was obvious we had a problem. Apparently there wasn't a spare spur from which our supply could be run. The only solution was to dig up the road and connect a new spur direct from the mains. I didn't think this was too much of a problem, until I realised it was expected that it would be me doing the digging. I didn't mind too much, until it was pointed out that the mains lay beneath a metre of concrete. I thought this was a little beyond my technical capability, being as I only had a shovel.

Alekos sympathised with my predicament and shook his head. He remembered that Andonis had had the same problem the previous year. I looked and could see where poor old Andonis had had to dig, but why oh why did he have to fill the damned thing in again with concrete! Hadn't they heard of manhole covers? Obviously not.

I asked Alekos to introduce me to the plumber and negotiated a price with him to undertake the whole job, from digging the hole, fitting the meter and connecting the pipe. Satisfied, we shook hands and agreed the work would be completed within the week. Suffice to say, two months later the job was completed!

With water now on tap, we could again concentrate upon developing the garden. Digging by the side of the house, we hit something solid. It was flat and large. Very large. Old foundations perhaps? Gradually, like archeologists we carefully brushed away the soil to a depth of half a metre. That must make it three or four thousand years old at least. Whatever it was, measured some three metres or more in diameter. Excited by our find, we fitted rocks around its circumference and made steps to it with some flat stones left over from the path. Hey presto. We had ourselves a sunken sun terrace, surrounded by flowers.

It was not until much later that Alekos laughingly told us that our 'find' was, in fact, the previous owner's cess pit!

Over the months everything in the garden began to grow. Huge Hybiscus were everywhere - mauve ones, salmon pink, others were white, red, some maroon, yellow and bright orange. Fuscias too grew in abundance, and Geraniums were absolutely everywhere. Magically, cuttings taken from the Geraniums rooted themselves and began to grow in a matter of days. The whole garden was a feast of colour. All we needed was a lawn.

We found a seed merchant in the back streets of Chania and bought ten kilos. The day after we spread the grass seed, we were alarmed to discover it was all moving. On closer inspection it was evident that the whole ant population of Afrata had arrived for the feast and was carrying off the spoils without even waiting for a doggy bag.

Back we went to the seed merchant.

Did he have anything to suggest? We were given a box of powder to sprinkle over the ground which would, he assured us, do the trick. There was however, one little drawback. The powder had an extremely pungent smell, which, if spilt onto clothes would be very hard to remove. Carefully we followed his instructions and while the ground looked as if snow had fallen, the ants no longer appeared interested and the seeds began to germinate within the week.

The longest of our boundary lines was marked by just a few stakes. To save any future disagreement, we felt it would be prudent to have Michylie build a wall.

One morning we were woken by his truck. Lumbering down the mountainside, it sounded a lot sicker than usual. In fact it was almost groaning. With a sigh it drew up outside. Looking out of the window I could see why the old vehicle had been struggling. It was piled high with breeze blocks and bags of cemenmt. If I had likened my meagre pathways to the Palace of Knossos, then this must surely rank as Afrata's Great wall of china.

Block after block was thrown off the rusting truck until a vast grey pile lay higgledy piggledy all over the ground. This was followed by the bags of cement - one of which burst as it landed heavily on the corner of one block.

Having emptied the tired old truck, Michylie jumped into the jalopy and was off again, to return two hours later with another load. This procedure was repeated yet again the following day.

Three days went by without him putting in another appearance and then, on the fourth day, he arrived, complete with hoe and shovel. Climbing over the vast pile of blocks, which now totally blocked the driveway, he strode to the boundary line and began to mark out lines for the foundation. By the end of the day he had dug a deep trench the entire length. The effort must have made him tired, because he needed a further three days to recuperate before showing up again.

By this time our survival was in jeopody. With building blocks to the left of us and a deep trench to the right, we were imprisoned. Supplies were running dangerously low. One of us needed to break out. I drew the short straw. Like a fugitive from Colditz, I managed to climb over the perimeter wall unseen, with shopping bag concealed beneath my tee shirt. As dusk fell, I returned, mission accomplished. We had provisions for a futher three days.

So it went on. Two days work. Three days off. Progress was slow, but gradually the wall was taking shape, until the final, eventful day arrived. It was completed. Well almost. Materials had run out and the wall ended jaggedly, with still a further metres of boundary line to go.

Eager to receive our enthusiastic congratulations for a fine job of work, Michylie proudly showed us his patented design, should we wish to add a trellis to the wall. This was unlikely as it already stood chest high. However, he had cemented a Coca Cola tin into the top of the wall every two metres, where a post could be set at any time in the future.

Whether or not, like the Great Wall of China, the Great Wall of Afrata is visible from outer space, I don't know, but along its entire fifty five metre length, when the sun is low, chinks of light shine through between each building block. Michylie's philosophy of why waste cement when it was so costly, meant two handsome dollops of mortar - one to the left and another to the right of every block was more than sufficient.

With sun beams playing through the chinks, it almost looked a picture. After all, it was the longest wall ever built in Afrata, altough perhaps it would not match the longevity of its twin in China.

This was not the only building work we required. The roof on the house was originally asbestos and the ceiling beneath was of wooden lattice work. Because the roof sloped only slightly, there was a problem of leaks during heavy rainfall. As Michylie was only a cement man, we used a local builder from Kolimbari to undertake the work of constructing a new roof. We couldn't bear to live there while the old roof was ripped off and all the mess it was going to involve, and so we returned to England while the work was completed.

Upon our return, we had a lovely red tiled roof and inside, all the ceilings were immaculate in a bright, white, tongue and grooved finish. We also had lodgers. My worst nightmare.

Rats.

Lying in bed, I was awoken at four in the morning by a scurrying and scratching and then a wild scampering round and around - like a playful dog having a funny half hour. It sounded as heavy as a cat. God. What did they feed their rats on in this neck of the woods? Fearing the ceiling would be brought down, I was all for abandoning ship and jumped out of bed. Pauline is one of those people who need eight hours sleep and most definitely she was not going to be short changed in her slumbers by a hyperactive fool of a rat. I was not so stout hearted.

The shuffling broke out again. This time it was right above my head. Bravely, I reached up and gave the ceiling a little tap to frighten the beast. It was not scared. Suddenly, what seemed like falling masonry casquaded down onto the ceiling. I ducked. I listened. All was quiet on the Western front.

In the stillness, the native hunter eased himself from the bed and stealthily crept from one room to the next, pausing every few seconds, head raised, nostrils flared, straining to catch the slightest sound.

What was that?

A long, rasping rattle and a slow grunt made me turn with a start. With relief I realised it was Pauline, back in the land of nod.

In the spare room I made to stand on the bed, when the ceiling above me creaked. Quietly I stood on the mattress, drunkenly swaying to and fro - the springs making me lurch unsteadily. There it was again. A scuffling noise. I looked out of the window. The sun was dawning and the morning was perfectly still. - except for the olive tree outside. One branch was swaying. Horrorstruck I knew, but like a rabbit caught in the headlight of a car, I could not avert my gaze. There it was. A huge great black rat ambling out of the tree and along the washing line. It stopped on my pants. Please, please - but my prayer was too late. My pants were marked. I shuddered. I could never wear them again. Sensing someone was there, it stared straight at me, its eyes glinting with evil malice and then it was gone, into the tree.

Directly the supermarket was open, I was down the mountain

to Kolimabari like a shot. Returning with my booty, I prepared the Mother of all offensives. This was war. Halving a large tomato, I piled each piece high with poison and then surreptitiously placed one on the wall, by the tree and the other on the corner of the roof, where the clothes line was tied.

I monitored the situation over the next few days, but the beast obviously didn't like tomatoes, as they remained untouched. Perhaps I had underestimated the foe. More deviousness was required.

You could set your watch by it. Every morning, on the dot of four thirty, a thump, thump, thump, could be heard as it limbered up for the day with a few aerobic excercises before leaving the house. I decided to catch it out. Setting my alarm before it woke up, I threw on my dressing gown and went outside. It was still dark, but soon a halo of light appeared behind the ridge above the house and gradually the darkness became grey. Sitting there on the garden wall, with the cold damp air swirling around my nether regions, I waited for the loathsome creature to appear. The greyness gave way to a golden pink hue and still I sat there motionless, my eyes fixed on the roof. An hour later, concerned I might suffer from being seated for so long on the damp wall, Afrata's great white hunter decided to call it a day.

For three days I sat there. Not once did the animal have the decency to put in an appearance. Yet, as soon as I returned indoors, the rat would pull on its hob nailed boots and begin to limber up.

There was only one, sure fire solution. Cement.

Day six of Operation Exterminator saw me shaking at the top

of a ladder. This was mainly due to the fact that I had followed the old Cretan proverb - 'poverty creates art'. I made myself a traditional village style ladder, built of wood, wide at the base and narrow at the top. Unfortunately it was only two metres high, which necessitated me having to stand, rather nervously, on the top rung, with my face tight against the pebble dashed wall. With a large dollop of cement on a board, held in my outstretched left hand and a trowel in my outstretched right, I clung like a limpet. I didn't feel particularly safe, but it was a haven compared to when I had to reach across to deposit cement on my trowel. With bottom waving dangerously in mid air and my face glued to the pebble dash, I attempted to fill the gap beneath each roof tile, which gave access to the roof space.

After five minutes of dropping more mortar than I managed to trowel into place, I resorted to using handfuls of cement. I toiled throughout the day.

A toot, toot, heralded six thirty as Michylie's truck approached.

Seeing this fool of an Englishman, standing on the top rung of a too short, rickety ladder, attempting to apply cement a metre above his head - he slowed down and stopped - I don't know whether out of curiousity, or concern, but he gave a cheery wave. Forgetting I was perched so precariously, I gave a devil may care wave in return and nearly lost my balance. One leg pedalled furiously in mid air, as I dropped my board of mortar. The guilty hand, set almost solid in cement, grabbed hold of the ladder. For seconds I hung on grimly. For a minute I was certain I was going to fall, but the moment passed.

"Yassou, Michylie," I shouted, in a voice a tiny mite higher than normal.

"Yassou. Ti kaneis," he replied, a wide grin appearing beneath his flowing moustache.

I called down, "I'm sealing the roof. When I reach the last hole, I'm going to drop poison into the roof space."

Michylie looked concerned and shouted something in Greek, which I did not understand. Seeing the blank expression on my face, he attempted to repeat his comments in a mixture of Greek and English. "To pontikos, tha fartei - bad food - he smile."

This quantum leap in languages was beyond me. "Smile? Yiati?"

"Bad food. Pontikos he smile."

I laughed as I deciphered the correct translation and explained as best I could, the difference between 'smile' and 'smell'!

Finally the job was done. Everywhere was sealed as tight as a drum - all except the final hole. Through this I had poked a dozen tablets of poison. Roland was an unwanted guest. He could leave, or be entombed. If he opted for the latter, he would just have to 'smile'. Besides, I reasoned, he would only smell for a few days surely. In my eyes this was a small price to pay.

During the next couple of days there was considerable activity up in the loft, but by sheer animal cunning and native guile, I discovered Roland went out on the tiles every night at eight thirty. He was as good as mine. With ladder and cement at the ready, I hid behind the old olive tree. It was 8.28. Only two minutes to go. It was dusk and difficult to see, but there, silhouetted against the sky, Roland's head could be plainly seen. Suddenly, behind me, came a blood curdling shriek and a loud fluttering noise. It was a large owl. The bird, with undercarriage down, skimmed the roof to, plainly aimimg to get an early takeaway. Roland was obviously nobody's fool and ducked back into the roof. The thwarted owl soared up and away, looking for another tempting morsel.

Meanwhile, back on the ground, the great white hunter stood motionlessly, eyes fixed, staring and waiting for his adversary to appear. Five minutes went by and it was now almost nightime. Suddenly there he was. The long snout sniffed at the air, searching for any strange smell. The ears tuned into any faint noise likely to herald danger. Undetected, I watched as the beast twisted his body and in a flash was out and top of the roof.

"Geromino," I shouted and ran with all my acoutrements to the side of the house. Shinning up the ladder, ignoring the way it was swaying, I slapped cement into the one, last remaining gap. I had won. The house was safe. Man had yet again conquered the alien foe.

That night I awoke at four thirty in the morning. Like Freddy, the nightmare on Afrata Street had returned.

The job was done. The house was a tomb. It could not escape. The last rat had stayed at home. I lay there, listening to the scampering hither and thither above me. Then I heard the chewing. No! It was going to eat its way through the ceiling!

For three days I listened to the terrible noises, as they grew weaker and weaker. The next day there were mewing sounds and the scampering was getting slower and slower. On the fifth day there was only silence.

It was the law of the jungle - survival of the fittest. Man once again reigned supreme.

Three weeks later the rat smiled.

CHAPTER 8

It's not all sun

While the island is radiant in Spring and sultry in Summer, the Autumn and Winter are times when Crete belongs to its people.

Making ready for Winter, we arrived from England via Athens with luggage which seemed to weigh far more than the usual hundredweight I was used to lugging around. In each case lay an oil filled electric radiator - essential heating for a village house which was built to withstand hot Summer days and not cold, damp Winters.

Scandinavians cannot understand why the British don't prepare for the effects of snow. We shrug and say, "well, it's only for such a short time. It's just not worth bothering about." We then grumble when it snows and traffic grinds to a halt and deliveries are delayed. The Cretans are the same. "Winter lasts for such a short time - it can be really warm even in January. Why do we need all your central heating?" They then grumble when their houses become damp and they huddle around a single wood stove trying to keep warm.

The weather was warm in January when we arrived at the house, back from England, but a cold dampness greeted us from inside, when we opened the door. The radiators were going to be indispensible. That night we battened down the hatches and drew the curtains. I put on the CD, while Pauline had a shower. Since the installed hot water system required rubber gloves to be worn, when showering, as a safety precaution; we had fitted an electric shower, brought over from England. To make the bathroom a little more cosy, there was also a heat'n'light.

"Can you make a cup of tea darling," called Pauline?

Suddenly the CD broadcast a series of plaintiff scratches, before seizing up altogether. The lights dimmed to a level that candles would have seemed floodlights.

"Ahhhhhhhhhhhhhhhhhh," came a cry from the bathroom, like an animal in pain. "The water's like ice. What the hell have you done?"

Putting on the electric kettle was the straw that broke the camel's back, because we were the last house on Afrata's electric supply, by the time power reached us, it was pretty ropey, being highly suseptible to the useage made on it by other houses up the line.

In a case such as this a sublime approach was called for. With the sensitivity of a maestro conducting a symphony, I strode towards one radiator and slowly turned down the thermostat. In concert the lights grew to their full power. Adjusting the second radiator raised Dire Straits to a higher fi and a "that's better," signalled that all was well on the shower front. Unfortunately we had to wait for tea.

In the depths of our winter we did not relish the idea of being warm, at the sacrifice of having to sit in the dark, or, even worse, the alternative of having our creature comforts denied us. There was just not enough electricity to go round. It seemed the villagers didn't mind, as their lifestyle hadn't yet included a mode of living which depended on the support of a wide array of electric gadgetry.

The solution was to go village and buy a 'fornos'.

The next day we drove down to Tavronitis, some ten kilometres away, on the road to Chania. We had been told there was a workshop there where a craftsman built wood stoves, that were the finest in all Crete.

Perhaps we should have remembered that impressions gained from glowing descriptions, occasionally fell a little short, in reality. We pictured a showroom of the finest stoves. Beautiful fires, with intricate Victorian embellishments of filligree and patterns. Wrong. Here, the finest means strongly made and solidly functional.

We discovered the 'showroom'. It was the muddy back yard of a work shop. Here, two men were welding in the gloomy interior of a rusting, corrugated building. Neither used goggles. As they laboured intently, shafts of brilliant blue light and snorting orange sparks projected their elongated shadows on the walls behind.

"Yanni," I called, the name I was given to ask for.

"Ela," came a reply from the eldest, as he stopped welding, the blue oxyacetylene flame still roaring by his side.

Explaining we were looking for a wood stove, he directed us back out into the yard. There, looking very forelorn, like a miniature Thomas the tank engine, stood a relic from years gone by. However, Yanni assured us it had only just been built the week before, but with nightime damp, the steel was now a little rusty, but only the top surface - just a mere covering that would easily rub off. This was not a problem, we were informed. Yanni prided himself on being a craftsman and his reputation was such that he would paint the stove before it was delivered.

"Would that be in fireproof paint," I ventured to ask?

"Vair, vair - certainly," came the indignant reply.

The stove was basically a steel rectangular box with legs. On closer inspection it seemed the design features were loosely based upon a traditional Aga cooker. However, looks can be deceiving and apart from the initial thought, there the resemblance stopped. On the left there was a hinged lid, beneath which lay a compartment for the fire. An optional extra was included, which consisted of a steel rectangular plate with a large hole cut out of the middle. Slotted into place above the fire, a useful hot plate was created - or so we thought. We discovered later, that flames licking at the bottom of a sooted saucepan leave a lot to be desired when it comes to the washing up! Beneath the fire a labour saving drawer allowed easy access to remove the ashes. To the right was the oven itself, with an integral fixed shelf. The whole thing must have weighed some seventy kilos or more and to facilitate ease of carrying, a handle had been thoughtfully welded on each side. Not for us the boring perfection of mass manufacture. Here was indeed a true edifice of craftsmanship - albeit not a masterpiece. Nothing was level, or married up with its counterpart opposite - but it did have character - and we loved it.

Paying the asking price, we arranged for it to be delivered before six that evening.

It was four in the afternoon and I had already knocked the

hole out in the wall and cemented in the galvanised chimney flue. Outside it proudly ran two metres up the side of the house, crowned by an 'H' to prevent rain falling down the chimney.

Alekos was curious. He had heard all the banging as he walked the sheep down to their pen. Leaving them to graze outside, he came in to investigate. Congratulating us on having the sense to buy a traditional fornos, he was a little contemptious of the position it was going in.

"You must run the pipe into the middle of the room. The fornos will be much better there, for you will have the heat all around. Only the walls will be warm if it is put there, in the corner," and he shrugged, completely at a loss to understand how on earth we could be so silly.

The fact that we did not want a long metal chimney flue strung out across the lounge was something that would not occur to him. Practicality and efficiency was everything. Aesthetics were a luxury that had little value in his eyes. He was concerned that we would rue the day if we failed to heed his advice. Gently we explained to our old friend that we preferred the fornos in the corner, but his opinon had certainly given us food for thought and we would seriously consider what he had said. At this he smiled, happy that perhaps we would not be folish after all. Waving us goodbye, he walked down the path to retrieve his flock of sheep which were grazing noisily in the road.

Hoping we would not offend Alekos by ignoring his advice, we waited for him to go, before setting off down to the beach in the car to collect a great pile of driftwood. Now, everything was ready. All we needed was the fornos.

At six thirty a chug, chug, chug heralded the arrival of the delivery truck and there, in all its glory, stood our fornos. It had been painted and the silver glinted in the setting sun, a pink halo surrounding this testimony to craftmanship in metal. Two of us lifted the beast down and with a huffing and a puffing, we struggled up the garden path, before finally depositing the huge metal creation beneath the galvanised flue sticking out from the wall. Waving the driver goodbye, I looked down at my hands. They were silver. The paint was still wet, but this was a small price to pay for the luxury of warmth.

Eagerly I fitted the connecting pipe. Now, everything was ready. As I never qualified as a boy scout, the ceremony of lighting the inaugral fire fell to Pauline - self appointed pack leader. With paper, kindling and three logs, a fire was soon roaring away. Within minutes the metal quickly heated up to furnace level and, as the paint became hot, so it began to give off grey, noxious fumes. With eyes streaming, we fought our way outside to shiver in the garden, until the cool night air brought some comfort. As our teeth began to chatter, we had little choice. Was it going to be death by hypothermia or asphysixia? After due consideration we felt it more preferable to die in the warm.

For the next three hours we sat there, huddled together, while the stove roared away, to little effect. With the front door and windows all wide open, the furnace-like heat selfishly rushed outside to meet the cold night air, leaving us to breathe in its wake, toxic fumes with tears streaming down our face. Occasionally it all got too much and we were forced to make a dash for the garden to resuscitate ourselves. By midnight the fornos had burned itself out and there was now some semblance of breatheable air inside the house. Before crawling into bed, I glanced at our new purchase in the corner. With its mask of silver paint now bubbled and blistered, it resembled a sad, de- masked Phantom of the Opera, scarred and deformed.

The next day I wire-brushed away the last remnants of silver paint. Like a peeling skin, the final loose flakes fluttered to the floor to leave our fornos pristine in its birthday suit of shiny metal. Declared cleansed of toxic paint, Brown Owl stepped in with her firelighters to stoke up the fire to furnace proportions. As the logs burned, so the whole house became as warm as toast. Putting the oven through its paces, the delectable aroma of a traditional Greek dish began to waft through the air, as it gently braised in the fornos - succulent leg of lamb, surrounded by potatoes, wallowing in stock, local oil and lemon juice. Undoubtedly - this was indeed the finest wood stove to be had.

With continual forages to maintain our supply of wood and exercising supreme control of the electricity supply by rationing the use of appliances, we managed to live in warmth and comfort.

That is, until the hurricane.

It was two in the morning and we were soundly sleeping, when an almighty crash brought us to semi-consciousness. Flapping my hand around in the darkness trying to trace the lamp I knew was there somewhere, I half fell out of bed as lightning lit up the whole room. I awoke with a start. I was all wet. Surely I hadn't yet reached the age where I was becoming incontinent? Hell. I must have drunk twenty pints at least to flood the floor to this degree. Another crash of thunder banished all slumber from my mind. With relief I realised it wasn't me. We were flooded. But how? The house wasn't by the sea or a river. Where was it coming from?

"Look! There's water coming through the window. Quick. Go outside and close the shutter."

It was all very well Pauline directing operations from beneath a warm duvet, but it was hell out here. I kissed her goodbye and made my way to the front door, splashing through the water which had by now run into the lounge. Throwing the door open, like Scott of the Antarctic I walked out into the storm, perhaps never to be seen again.

Sheet lightning illuminated the whole garden. The wind was violent, driving the rain into stinging needles. I stood there on the verandha, my dressing gown hanging around me like a saturated nappy. The howling wind was so fierce it was painful to open my eyes. Bent into the hurricane, I tried to walk, but remained stationary, as if I was going the wrong way down an escalator. With difficulty I staggered down the steps and was hit by a tidal wave sweeping down the garden path. The wind tore at my dressing gown, like a rampant poltergist, threatening to untie the knot that lay between me and some semblence of decency. Branches of the olive tree scythed madly through the air, blindly attempting to prevent me from passing. With arm up to protect my face, I pushed through the foliage to reach the bedroom window.

The darkness momentarily vanished as lightning flashed and a demented figure stood before me, hands clawing the air, its mouth moving uncontrollably. In the deadly silence that followed, before the deafening crash of thunder, a voice could be heard calling - "can you bring the washing in?"

Slamming the shutters shut, the peal of thunder drowned my reply.

I made my way around the house, fighting to close all the

wooden shutters as the wind struggled to keep them open. In common with village houses, the roof did not have guttering and rivers of rain poured off in a roaring waterfall. With little overhang from the roof, the savage wind was blowing a torrent of rainwater against the window, and the sheer volume was just too much for each crack and leak to bear, with the result that countless rivulets were running down inside. Reaching the last pair of shutters I tried to close them, but the wood was so swollen it was impossible. Giving the whole thing up as a bad job, I left them swinging wildly in the wind. Job done, I followed instructions and brought in the washing.

Silhouetted against the lightning, washing like a fig leaf held over my nether regions, dressing gown billowing out like a cloak, I stood there in the front doorway like a bedraggled rat. A high pitched scream was just discernable above the hurricane howling outside. Dropping the saturated bundle, I ran to the spare bedroom. Water on the tiled floor was as slippery as ice and like a gross parody of Torville and Dean, I slipped, tumbled and glided across the room to make a grand entrance. Sadly my acrobatic glory was short lived. With shins colliding with the foot of the bed, I ended facedown, spreadeagled on the bed.

"Look. At the window. Look!"

I looked and there clinging to the window was a large bedraggled rat. Given the choice of hurricane weather, or two humans waving and shouting at you, probably the latter seemed very small potatoes. Summoning up every ounce of courage, I banged on the window. It looked at me so dolefully. I knew. I'd been out there. It looked at me like a child ordered to bed, plaintifully begging to stay up for just another five minutes. I gave the window another bang. It looked at the water swirling below, gave me a look as if to say, "you dirty rat," and jumped down into the darkness. This was just as well, because the wind suddenly tore at the shutter, slamming it into the window frame like a demolition weight and back out again into the night. If the rat hadn't taken that moment to abandon ship he would have become ratatouille, squashed against the glass. I was glad I had saved his life. I wouldn't have relished cleaning the window.

Still the water continued to run down the wall, despite our building a flood barrier. No. We didn't exactly have sandbags. Again following the old Cretan maxim - poverty creates art - Pauline had constructed huge sausages out of kitchen roll, toilet rolls and tissues - and very attractive they looked too. However, it was soggy useless. There was only one solution. For the rest of the night, like two privates on guard duty, straight out of Dad's Army, we stood there armed with a mop and bucket. As soon as a rivulet swelled to a size ready to run under furniture, it was battered with a mop.

For two hours we stood our ground, repelling the flood, until day dawned. By eight the battle had been won. We emerged from our shelter to greet the world outside. A scene of havoc met us. Our garden table and chairs were scattered everywhere, branches were broken off trees, garotting innocent flowers and in the midst of all this carnage stood a sheep quietly munching away.

"Kali mera, kako pethee."

Alekos entered the garden smiling, walking stick in hand, a baseball cap on his head and a bright yellow cycling cape over the rest of him. He had been wandering the mountain all night, looking for his sheep. The hurricane had blown down an old tree which had crashed onto the fence surrounding the pen, leaving a wide gap for the animals to escape. With the one in the garden, he only had another four to find. With a call of "Ela, ela, ne, ne," the sheep calmly followed him out of the garden, back home.

Apart from the water problem, we were pleased the house had stood up so well to the hurricane. The roof was undamaged and apart from having to clean up the garden, there was only one piece of repair work to do. The shutters which had become badly swollen needed to be planed down in order for them to shut properly. Unfortunately there was one problem. I did not possess a plane.

There was only one person I knew who may be able to help - Makis - the Arthur Daley of Tavronitis.

I drove the fifteen minutes to Tavronitis, where I found Makis sitting beside his petrol pump. He was a short podgy man, with a wild, bushy beard and piercing brown eyes. I had never seen him in anything other than tee shirt, shorts and sandals.

"Yassou. Ti karnis," he waved.

Within moments he produced two plastic beakers and a bottle of tskouthia. After chewing the fat over a drink or two, or three, he offered me a banana. There was nothing unusual in this. Makis grew them. The Makis empire also sold petrol, had a shop behind his pump that sold anything and everything, while next door he ran a souvlaki, fast food cafe. In addition, he also grew tomato plants in plastic bags which he hawked around all the villages.

Makis had several friends around the world, including an airline pilot, who had all brought him different varieties of banana plants. With a government grant he had built a vast greenhouse and was soon in business. All was going well. Every morning he would take his dog and spend an hour or two tending his plants, until, one morning, he noticed teethmarks on the lower leaves of one tree. The dog had been chewing them. He scolded the dog and threatened to punish him if he ever did it again.

Each day he inspected the trees and discovered more teethmarks. Worse. The first tree attacked by the dog was now showing signs of losing all its fruit. Makis was very angry. The dog was losing him money. Finally, after a week, with two more trees now dying he was beginning to face ruination as a banana grower. Daunted by the prospect, he lost his tether, took the dog out and shot it dead.

Two days later, as if the animal had come back to haunt him, he discovered another tree with teethmarks on its leaves. Puzzled, he telephoned the agricultural office in Chania, who confirmed the marks were not canine, but a bug which could easily be irradicated by spraying. It was not his poor dog at all!

Trying to keep a straight face at this example of rough justice, Cretan style, we solemly toasted man's best friend, whose only mistake had been to have Makis as its owner.

Finally, after an hour, Makis eventually rummaged around at the back of his shop and produced a plane. Promising to return it the following day, I bade him farewell and returned up the mountain to complete my chores.

In our part of Crete the weather in winter is not always cold and damp - although when it does rain, boy does it rain. January can be a lovely month, with sunny days and bright blue sky. It is also the time to pick olives. Being a farmer with nine trees of my own, I can appreciate the back breaking work this involves. Why, sitting in the garden, a drink by my side, I have nothing but sympathy for those who own hundreds!

In one grove next to the house, there are about twenty trees and the whole family are commandered to help pick the crop. Plastic bags, all sewn together, are laid around each tree to form a great carpet. The men climb up into the branches and beat each tree with stout sticks. Below, women and children sift through the fallen leaves and twigs to pick out the olives, which are then bagged up. To harvest just one tree takes perhaps two or three hours and that tree will yield perhaps fifty or sixty kilos. You can imagine the time and effort it takes to pick hundreds of trees - many of which appear to grow in the most inaccessible of places.

Gradually, for some, technology is beginning to reduce a little of the effort involved.

As I sat there, Michylie, his wife Sophia and their three children all arrived. A generator was brought into the garden, the sacks were laid around one tree and a strange looking attachment was linked to an air hose running from the generator. The air was suddenly filled with a raucous whining and Michylie began to flail the tree with what looked like a glorified strimmer.

Within fifteen minutes the tree's fruit lay on the ground, where the Papatherakis family picked out the leaves and twigs and filled a fifty kilo bag. All nine trees were completed in five hours flat. The nine bags were humped onto the back of Michylie's truck and off the family went to the next grove.

Families spend several weeks harvesting their olives and trucks are driven all over the mountain to collect the booty, before descending on Kolimbari to the local farmer's co-op. Here, each family's crop is weighed and then pressed to extract the oil. Sufficient for their own needs for the next year are taken and the balance is sold.

With subsidies being lost and payment for the harvest being delayed until May, the topic of discussion in the village for days on end is the miserly low price of their olives. Invariably the other topic of local discussion is politics. In Greece it is a legal requirement to vote and therefore this subject takes up many hours of mutual commiseration over the way the Government raises the price of bread or petrol - in fact the price of anything and everything.

It is in winter, when the Kafenio's door is tightly closed, and invariably there are six or seven people huddled round the fire of an evening, that many a lively discussion takes place.

A wodge of newspaper is wedged into the large round hole, high up in the wall, during the summer, but in the winter this is punched out and a four metre length of pipe is inserted. This protrudes outside, while the other end is held in place by a twisted loop of wire cemented into the solid ceiling. A vertical pipe connects with the horizontal, to form a chimney system seven metres long. The final piece of this Heath Robinson contraption is a 'somba' - basically a metal pipe on legs, with a higed lid on top through which lumps of tree are dropped in to keep the fire burning.

Almost to a man, the villagers vote Pasok - the Greek Socialist Party. Being English, it is presumed we must be 'capitalists' as all Western Europeans are rich. If I haven't cut through this thinking, then I have certainly made strides towards becoming an 'Afratianos'.

With the wind howling and not a star to be seen in the sky, I walked to the door of the Kafenio. Through the window I could see Alekos, Michylie, Nikos, Andonis and Stavros. Each was wearing a jacket stretched over a thick pullover beneath, making them look like swarthy Michelin men.

Roxannie was wearing a cardigan and around her shoulders she wore a knitted bed jacket, coyly fastened at the neck with a bow. She was crotcheting a beautifully worked bed cover, while the men were engaged in deep discussion.

All of them, like magnets, were drawn towards the somba, which radiated immense heat within a two metre circumference. Beyond this perimeter the temperature dropped alarmingly, as if it were the dark side of the moon.

Looming above the group perched a huge bird, like some prehistoric relic, its wings outstretched, with a span of more than two metres. Its eyes were like coalfires set above a fearsome crooked beak that could rip out the throat of a sheep in seconds. Thankfully it was stuffed. Michylie had shot it the previous summer as it swooped down to attack one of his flock. Now the thing could only eye the scraps left on the plates of unsuspecting tourists. However, the canaries, beside it, seemed not to worry, going by their continual chirping and whistling.

Throwing the door open, like a demented Incredible Hulk. OK, so a better description would be the Incredible Bulk - but at least I was dressed all in green - shirt, sweater and trousers.

"Pasok," I shouted, punching the air.

"Pasok," everyone shouted in return.

Alekos slapped me on the back and everyone congratulated me on wearing the party colours. It called for a drink. What did I think about all the petrol stations going on strike tomorrow?

Can you imagine being dressed in blue and entering your local, shouting, "Tory!" Would everyone ply you with drinks? I doubt it. Here in the village, we take our politics very seriously.

CHAPTER 9

Greek Philoxenia

As we have made friends and become accepted in the village, so we have enjoyed traditional Greek hospitality - 'philoxenia'. The word for stranger does not exist in the Greek language and, to the unitiated, it is a pleasant surprise to be invited into someone's home and be plied with a drink and a little something to eat.

In being accepted as part of village life, we have shared many enjoyable times with our friends and been witness to the sad loss of members of the community who have passed on.

One morning, on opening the door, there, on the step, stood a jam jar. This was not unusual in itself as we would often wake to find a gift of grapes, a bottle of wine or a bag of tomatoes left by a kind 'fairy'. However, this was a mite unusual. The lid was tightly screwed on and its contents were an unappetising sludge brown. Picking it up, I was surprised to find it was warm. Calling Pauline for a second opinion, we looked at the jar, wondering what it was and who had left this unusual present.

Apart from tadpoles, I reasoned that jam jars invariably contained something edible. Always one to investigate anything faintly resembling food, I gingerly unscrewed the top. I sniffed. It smelt sweet. Was it Cretan style meusli? Not being quite so adventurous, Pauline declined the offer to taste it first and would go no further than to give the jar a token sniff. Me? I reached for a spoon. Giving the contents a stir - it had the consistency of a brown semolina pudding - black bits, white bits and large cream lumps were disturbed from the hidden depths and dredged up to the surface. Scooping a spoonful, I viewed the assortment of unidentified chunks cemented into the brown sludge. From experience I know the tasting of unidentified lying objects is akin to wading into the sea. If you don't go under immediately, then you pussyfoot around for ages before summoning up sufficient courage. I looked at the spoonful for a split second before taking the plunge. Pauline's face screwed up as I put the spoon into my mouth. As the sludge drained away with a sweet taste similar to condensed milk, I ran my tongue over the assortment of 'bits' left behind. Pleasantly surprised, I discovered these were no more life threatening than raisins and almonds.

We learned later it was Roxannie who had left the jar.

Several weeks previously she had given us a bowl of 'koliva' - a dish of boiled wheat, mixed with nuts and raisins. This is a traditional symbol prepared at home and taken to the church to be blessed in memory of a deceased relative, forty days after their death. Roxannie's mother had just died in Chicago, aged ninety four.

It was now three months after her mother's death and, in the village, it was the custom to eat this preparation as a mark of remembrance. I didn't know about remembrance, but it was certainly a concoction I wouldn't forget.

Death in a small, religious community like Afrata, touches everyone with its grief.

A dear lady, who always went out of her way to greet us when we returned from England, invited us into her brand new house. For years she had lived in a tiny stone hovel with just three rooms, previously lived in by countless generations of her husbands family. Having brought up her children, who were now married, she lived for her new grandchildren. After proudly showing us their photographs, she would smile and hug the images to her bosom, closing her eyes as if to imagine they were really with her. Now, on the land next to the old family house, they had built a magnificent new home, with a huge balcony looking down the gorge and, what's more, a second floor upon which there was room for her son and his family.

She was so excited as she bustled around us one afternoon. We had been invited for coffee and for an hour we laughed and chatted, with her husband continually pulling her leg, as she giggled away like a schoolgirl. As we rose to leave, we were made to stop; we must take some peaches with us and she ran into the kitchen. After she had gone, her husband began to roar with laughter.

"We don't have any peaches," he explained. "She is so excited about the grandchildren coming tomorrow, she's mixed up. What's the betting she gives you a bag of apples. I picked them myself this morning."

As she returned, clutching a carrier bag, I made a great pantomime of looking inside and in mock amazement said, "aftee then eenai ta meela. Stin Elartha, ta leme 'rothakina' - then boreis na meleis Elenika?"

"These aren't apples. In Greece we call them peaches. Don't you speak Greek?"

She thrust the bag into my arms and with hands covering her face giggled uncontrollably.

We went back to England soon after and upon our return to Afrata six weeks later, I was walking up to the Kafenio to ogle passing tourists with Alekos, when I saw a lonely figure on the verandha of the new white house. I gave him a cheery wave. He looked a little older, mainly due to the beard he was now sporting and I made some comment about had he lost his razor. He smiled weakly and turned back into the house.

Relating this to Alekos, he patiently explained what had happened only a month ago. Our bearded friend had woken up one morning, to find his wife dead beside him. Apparently she had died in her sleep from a heart attack. As a sign of his love and respect, it was village tradition that a husband no longer shaved and grew a beard in memory of the partner he had lost in life.

It was a sad loss which I felt all the more, because the crass comment I had made, could not have helped his grief.

Right at the top of the village lives Nikos and his wife Argirula. Invited to come for coffee in the afternoon, we briskly set out on the fifteen minute walk. It was four o' clock and we were a little late. By the time we arrived, the steep gradient had taken its toll and we were puffing and panting. After all this exertion, we then discovered the garden gate was locked. A chain wound around the handle, and secured by a padlock, barred access. We slumped against the garden wall to catch our breath. I rattled the gate fruitlessly.

A voice bellowed from inside the house. "Perimenatai - wait."

Nikos was there.

We later discovered 'afternoon' in Greece applies to any time between five and eight o'clock! We had arrived a trifle early, waking Nikos and Argirula from their afternoon nap.

Nikos emerged, bleary eyed, his thick white hair tumbling down over his eyes. He was wearing a vest and a hastily pulled on pair of jeans. Barefoot he ran towards us, expressing his apologies. Unlocking the gate to let us in, he beckoned us to follow - "ela, ela." He led us to a table and chairs set out under a canopy of grape vines, and asked to be excused while he dressed.

The garden was a delight. Pathways and old stone walls had been painted over the years with layer upon layer of white lime. What were once rough and uneven surfaces, were now so smooth, it seemed as if thick cream had been poured over every stone.

Everywhere there were flowers and shrubs, a riot of colour, made all the more brilliant by the white walls creating a dazzling background. Besides the flowers, a lemon, orange and almond tree graced the courtyard. Terra cotta pots of all sizes and shapes were hap hazardly arranged, overflowing with flowering plants and herbs. A lush pomegranate tree created a natural arch leading to a large, white walled pit. It was here, every September, that the villagers assembled to tread the grapes.

Traditionally women are not allowed to take an active part, save to keep a constant supply of food and drink for the revellers. Participants sit on the wall, to have their feet washed and cleaned. They then swing themselves into the pit, enthusiastically treading the mound of grapes, some half a metre deep. As each man stomps around in a clockwise direction, they continually reach out to grab a drink held out to them, as they pass. Unlike a marathon, where the same thing happens, this was not water, but tskouthia!

As the grapes squelch and burst underfoot, the juice flows down through a plug hole in the centre of the pit, to a conduit leading directly into casks. As soon as the tramping presses them down, so more grapes are poured in out of great plastic bins. It is hard work and clothes quickly become splattered with juice. At last, as each tired participant struggles out of the pit, a sprig of sweet smelling 'vasiliko' - basil, is awarded him by tradition to wear behind his ear. A well earned token.

"Yassus pethee mou," Argirula greeted us, as she stepped out into the courtyard. She was a quiet, gentle lady with blue eyes and blonde hair. Her smiling face was at once welcoming, but flustered hands betrayed her nervousness as she aplogised for not having anything ready for our visit. I explained it was our fault for being early and that in England, afternoon means two or three o'clock. Nikos, who by then had joined us, laughed, his gold tooth glinting in the sunlight - "thie ee ora eenai tin mera etho - two o'clock is morning here!"

Their house was traditionally Cretan. The original building must have been some two hundred or more years old. Then, as family needs grew, so another part was added and again, sometime later, yet another. However, because the courtyard for most of the year serves as a place to eat, to entertain and, sometimes, when the nights are hot, even a place in which to sleep - it is looked upon as another room. Consequently the three doors to each part of the house open directly onto the courtyard. Thus, to go from one room to another, means first having to go outside.

Excusing herself, Argirula disappeared into the kitchen to prepare coffee. Nikos also got up and explained he would return in one moment.

Sitting in the immaculate courtyard garden, beneath the

canopy of vines shading us from the sun, still hot even at this time of day, it was hard to imagine this was not the nineteenth century - for little could have changed.

Nikos reappeared round the side of the house, clutching an armful of freshly picked almonds. Carefully laying them out on top of the wine pit wall, he picked up a stone and proceeded to shell them. On cue, Argirula came out from the kitchen, holding a tray of freshly baked biscuits, Greek coffees, accompanied by tumblers of ice cold water and a large dish of honey collected from local hives. Nikos tipped the shelled almonds into the dish of honey and invited us to try a spoonful. Needless to say, the combination was a delight - so much so, I ate nearly the whole dish.

The house was indeed very old and had belonged to Argirula's family for generations. She was one of ten children and had always lived in Afrata. Her brothers had long since gone to the mainland and while two sisters had married and still lived in the village, the remainder had moved and built their lives elsewhere on the island.

With coffee drunk, the nuts and honey eaten and a fair attempt at demolishing the plate of biscuits, we chatted and laughed the time away. Nikos felt it was time for something a little stronger than coffee and produced two cut glass decanters.

We were going to have a tskouthia tasting session!

The first sample was clear, yet with the merest hint of yellow. Mmmm. Deliciously warming with the kick of a mule.

The second was as clear as crystal. Mmmm. Deliciously warming with the kick of a mule.

The first was made from grapes and flavoured with saffron, which Nikos had picked from the mountainside. On reflection it was perhaps a shade more potent than the second. This had been made solely from mulberries and was marginally smoother. We sampled two or three glasses of each and the more we drank, the less difference there appeared to be!

Finally we bade our friends goodbye and weaved our way down the alleyway from their house, through the village and on down to home.

Telephone lines to the village are limited. We had applied for a 'phone two years previously and were still waiting. This was not unusual. A five year wait or more was not uncommon! Consequently we had to rely on messages being brought down to us. Friends would telephone the Kafenio and perhaps two or three hours later, one of the village children would inform us that someone had telephoned. Often no name was taken, or an indication given that the call would be returned. If we were lucky and the caller had made himself understood, confirming a time to call back, was this UK or Greek time? A two hour difference is quite a wait. Thus communication is invariably hit and miss.

One morning, a chatter of children's voices heralded an impending message. Giggling, they formed a group outside the garden gate, while Alekos, Michylie's eleven year old son walked importantly up the garden path to impart some vital information.

In schoolboy broken English - much the same level as my Greek - he relayed a message from his Mother.

"Will you please to our house come tonight? Says my mother and have the food with us?"

"Ti ora?"

"The hour she does not matter. Maybe the eight?"

Accepting the kind invitation, we told him to tell Sophia we would be pleased to come to dinner.

That evening, on the dot of eight, we arrived at Michylie and Sophia's home opposite the Kafenio. It is a large modern house, built by Michylie when he married Sophia. Due to the steep fall of the mountainside, the single storey building stands on stilts, making it level with the road, while below, a useful open basement area houses truck, car, rabbit hutches, wood for the winter, hay, cement mixer and other building supplies. We walked along the verandha to the kitchen door, to be met by Sophia. Smiling, she bade us welcome and ushered us to the table outside, where a decanter of tskouthia and a dish of nuts were laid. Apparently Michylie had been working in Kolimbari and was delayed, but only for half an hour or so.

Apologetically, Sophia excused herself as cooking in the kitchen required attention. I told her not to worry. It's surprising how time flies when you have your own decanter of tskouthia and a dish of nuts to pick at.

Eventually, with a toot, toot, the old Toyota pick up rounded the bend to reverse into the perilously narrow driveway, sloping down to beneath the house. Thirty seconds later a tousled head appeared over the verandha.

"Yassus," he called and held up a string of fish he had caught earlier that day. Going indoors he reappeared with a small barbecue; which he took to the side of the road and proceeded to light.

The chore completed, he now left us to shower and change.

We sat there gazing at the old village houses below us, moonlit beneath a huge diamond studded sky. As we sipped tskouthia, an owl's distant hoot echoed repeatedly, while from other verandhas, quiet murmers of conversation punctuated the air. Inside, Sophia could be heard, hard at work in the kitchen.

Within fifteen minutes, Michylie returned, having changed into fresh clothes, his curly hair still damp and droopy moustache freshly combed.

After joining us for a quick tskouthia, it was time for some earnest cooking. He brought out all the fish, freshly cleaned and checked the condition of the barbecue. Judging it was sufficiently hot, he laid the fish onto the grill, brushed them with olive oil and threw on a sprig of herbs, growing in a pot by the path. The heat was intense and soon the fish blistered, signifying it was time to turn them over for final cooking.

With the fish cooked to perfection, it was now time for dinner.

We stepped into the kitchen to a veritable feast and Sophia placing yet another platter on an already groaning table. She smiled and indicated we should be seated.

Michylie's wife was in her mid-thirties, a petite, softly spoken lady with wavy, shoulder length brown hair. She wore a demure expression, which hid an inate shyness, in contrast to the extrovert personality of her husband.

"Katsi, katsi," and at her request we sat down to eat. In front of us were bowls of fried potatoes and 'Horiatiki' - village salad

- topped with Sophia's delicious, own, homemade feta cheese. There was a platter of chicken and another of roast lamb, a plate of fried whitebait and a dish of 'horta' with roast goat meat. Where to start? Sophia handed out chunks of warm, crusty bread and Michylie poured glasses of the village wine. Let eating commence!

Sophia originally came from Heraklion, a good two hours drive away from Afrata. How on earth had they met?

Michylie had left school, completed his National Service in the army and had then returned to the village, where he settled down to a country life. His days were spent rearing sheep and goats, growing olives, grapes and vegetables, while interspersing these activities with building work in the village to supplement his income. By the time he reached his mid-twenties it was time to consider taking a wife. A friend recommended a girl in a village close to Heraklion. In fact it was less than a kilometre from the ancient site of Knossos. Taking the bull by the horns, one morning he made the long drive down the coast, with his friend, to meet this potential candidate for marriage. The subsequent consensus, after that first chaperoned meeting, resulted in them eventually becoming engaged.

Traditionally village couples met on recommendation from family or friends. If it was considered that marriage would be a suitable arrangement, then both families would meet to discuss this possibility. While the parents talked, the couple would leave the room. The hopeful husband would then divulge to the girl how much he earned, where they were to live and the standard of life she could look forward to. If these were to her satisfaction, then she would agree to marriage and the suitor would return to the families to formally ask the girl's father for his daughter's hand in marriage.

Come the great day, the Groom's parents pay for everything - from all the wedding costs, the Bride's dress and jewellery - even their house. The Bride's parents give their daughter a dowry, which, depending on rescources, could be land, or everything needed to make the house a home - such as furniture, cooking utensils, linen and electrical appliances.

I was now visibly wilting. The food had been so good. I hadn't paced myself. The Dinner had been a marathon and I had come off the starting blocks like a sprinter, filling my plate with everything that was going. I foolishly believed that what was on the table was everything we were due to eat. Wrong!

First the barbecued fish were served. In my haste to devour what was on the table, I had forgotten all about them. There were four large Red Mullet - one each.

Next, Sophia served four lobsters, each one broken down for easy devouring.

As if this wasn't enough, she then set to and fried about two dozen savouries - Calatsoonia. These are tiny, bite size filo pastry parcels, and contained Sophia's homemade cheese with herbs. Fresh from the pan, dipped in honey, it was manna from heaven cooked by an angel.

Still there was more. Vast wedges of sweet tasting watermelon and a dish of Paklava - tiny pastries with nuts and honey. I have never in my life eaten so much. I was well and truly stuffed.

Spreading his hands at the emptied dishes and plates, Michylie smiled. Everything we had eaten and drunk had been his own produce. He had even caught the lobster and fish himself.

The convenience of supermarkets and processed foods have not yet readily reached the confines of our wonderful village.

I looked forward to the walk home. It was downhill all the way to my bed, but at least the short exercise would ease the bulk of the concentrated bum bag on my fast expanding waistline.

And then Greek 'philoxenia' came to the fore in the guise of an Army keep fit training course. We couldn't leave without taking a huge watermelon - and a bag of goodies from Michylie's vegetable garden.

Such kindness you could die from.

Waving a fond farewell, we staggered down the road. The seven kilo weights on each arm worked like a medieval torture rack. Gradually the vegetables became heavier and my arms became longer. A small price to pay for such an evening and nothing to the friendship we had enjoyed.

CHAPTER 10

The Kafenio

Over the years, the clearing in the midst of the olive groves, where our house was built, has gradually become eroded as trees have stretched out their branches. Consequently it has become hidden from unsuspecting tourists.

One day Pauline and I left home to have lunch at the Kafenio with Alekos and Roxannie. It was October 28th - a national holiday commemorating the route of the Italian army by Greece during the Second World War.

Turning out of our drive, we saw a man with yellow trousers and a bum bag standing with his back to us. A rustle in the bushes signified he was not alone. Obviously believing there was nobody around and being away from any houses, they had felt the urge to answer the call of nature.

Adopting the maxim - I've started so I'll finish - he gave an embarassed, yet cheery wave, turning and keeping his back to us as we walked past. Looking down at his wife crouched in the bushes, I gave a friendly, "yassou." From her rather undignified position, she managed a rather watery smile and replied, "gutten tag."

When we arrived at the Kafenio, everyone thought it was hilarious when we told them. Alekos wanted to know whether I had bent down for a better view to say "yassou?" Nikos felt he ought to go down to the olive grove to turn off the irrigation, as it had now been watered. Imagine everyone's face when the couple appeared at the Kafenio half an hour later.

They were German and both in their sixties. Recognising us, they smiled - much to everyone's amusement - and ordered two beers and a salad. As the television was on, its magnetic appeal drew the attention of everyone there. Especially so as the programme being broadcast was a concert of Cretan music.

Working out in my mind, I calculated the couple would probably have been in their late teens, early twenties during the war. As the two tourists rose to leave, it coincided with the end of the concert. Obviously Nikos knew nothing of the Fawlty Towers programme and in particular the - "Don't Mention It To The Germans" - episode. Using the remote control, he flicked through the channels. Suddenly, there was the face of Hitler in a Greek war documentary. The German visibly stiffened and for a moment I thought he was going to salute and give a "seig heil."

Nikos grinned mischieviously and changed channels, but the damage had been done. Flustered, the tourists bade us all, "auf weidersein," and left.

The Kafenio is at the hub of the village - and the place where everyone stops for a chat or a coffee. One evening, sitting with Alekos and Michylie, a shout from Andonis interuppted our conversation. It was dark, apart from the light above us on the Kafenio wall. Andonis' house lay below us, and because of the steep fall of the mountain, the building couldn't be seen from where we sat.

"Ti," shouted Alekos to his older brother?

Again the disembodied voice shouted up to us. Michylie instructed Georgos, his youngest son, to run down to his great-uncle.

"What is it," I asked?

I was told to wait and see. Intrigued I waited for Georgos' head to pop up by the side of the road, and as he ran over to us, I saw he was clutching a paper parcel.

"Afto eenai poli oraio," said Alekos, taking out his knife. Laying open the parcel, it was evident this was indeed a gourmet's delight - an appetising grey mound of meat, which defied description. Indeed, it was not exactly clear as to what part, or even from which animal it had originated from. Alekos carefully cut the meat into mouth-size pieces and offered me an appetising morsel on the end of his knife. Forever one to taste first and suffer the consequences after, I ate it to find the taste was very like lamb, but slightly gamey.

Finishing the appetiser, Alekos offered me a larger piece, saying this is the best tasting part.

"Afto eenai ee katseeka - this is goat," I asked?

"Ne," came the answer, "afto ...," and Michylie demonstrated which part by pointing to himself.

What I was eating was a traditional Cretan dish - boiled throat of goat - and what's more, the appetising morsel I was about to eat was the lower lip! Oh well. In for a drachma, in for a pound. The texture reminded me of a cat's tongue and it tasted of very gamey, mutton. It was soft, but one piece was also extremely chewy. I excused myself and removed the offending part, to find what was so unchewable was in fact the gums!

"Ela na sou po." Again the voice of Andonis boomed up to us. Again Georgos was despatched to bring back another treat.

It was the fish course.

This time the parcel contained sardellas - similar to sardines, but cured in salt, which Alekos removed by washing the fish and soaking them in wine to remove all the salt. Putting them into a dish, swimming with olive oil, they were then served for our delictation. Because of the curing process, the bones were edible and therefore the whole fish could be eaten. I must admit I drew the line at the head and tail and removed these, much to the chagrin of my eating pals.

Life at the Kafenio was always a place of jovial hilarity, through the continual bantering between Roxannie and Alekos.

One morning we arrived to discover Alekos sitting dismally outside the locked Kafenio.

"It is ten thirty and I have no coffee. I am locked out of my own house, because my wife has a foolish idea," and he spread his hands, shrugging his shoulders with resigned acceptance.

Looking through the window, a strange sight greeted me. There was Roxannie holding a large mop, painting the high ceiling from a huge vat of white paint. Initially there wouldn't have been a problem, but the longer she painted, so gravity began to exert its influence and the saturated mop started to exude great globules of paint, which slowly trickled down the handle over her hands. In addition, with Roxannie's energetic waving of her 'brush', paint was being splattered everywhere. Consequently, she was now covered from head to toe in white. In order to see, she would remove her glasses every five minutes and make two holes in the paint covered lenses.

I remembered I had something packed away in the house which would be just perfect for Afrata's Michaelangelo. Within five minutes I was back and tapped on the door. Believing it was Alekos trying to get in to make a cup of coffee, she ignored me. More persistant banging gained her attention. Shuffling through the paint sodden newspapers covering the floor, she opened the door.

"Sygnomie, Michylie, emastai kleesta," she smiled wearily, "vafo to kafenio."

I commiserated with her that painting was hard work and she needed a break to rest for a few minutes. Leading her outside to sit by Alekos, I offered to make them both a cup of coffee and if she was good - very good, and did not argue with Alekos, I would give her a gift. Intrigued, she sat there excitedly while I went to brew two Greek coffees on the gas stove at the back of the Kafenio.

After fifteen minutes, when they had finished, I gave Roxannie her present, with instructions to go inside and not to come out until after she had opened the package. Excitedly she ran into the Kafenio, while we sat outside in the sun waiting. A shriek from inside signalled the present had been opened. Giggles and laughter, with intermittent grunts and wheezes could be heard. Five minutes elapsed and then the door was flung open. Roxannie stood there, mop held in one hand like a spear, the other on her hip, wearing the outfit I had given her - a plasticised paper overall and hood.

"Torra, eimai mia astronaut," she grinned. The overalls covered her totally except for nose, mouth and the proverbial glasses.

Processed foods were frowned upon by many of the village women, who were steeped in traditional ways, taught them by their mothers. Likewise, whatever Roxannie cooked was always fresh that day, be it meat from the pork butcher in Tavronitis, or fish from Kolimbari.

Pasta was something that Roxannie refused to buy.

So it was, one August morning, that we found her standing at a table inside the Kafenio, up to her arms in flour. Lifting a huge pitcher, she poured fresh sheep's milk into a bowl and added six newly laid eggs, whereupon she proceeded to make a dough. After several minutes of powerful kneading, when it had reached just the right consistency, she cut off a large lump and spread the table with flour. Gently she rolled the dough out. Proudly she reached down to the chair by her side and removed the tea towel which was covering... a gleeming pasta machine.

Every year since she was a tiny girl, helping her mother, Roxannie had made pasta. It was always cut by hand then, but now modern technology had arrived in the shape of this wonderful machine.

The table she was working at, left a lot to be desired in its construction, being both wobbly and out of square. However, the wonderful machine was duly ensconced, its bolt firmly secured and tightly clamped to the table.

Cutting the dough into strips, she loaded the pasta into the machine with one hand, while the other turned a handle feeding the dough through the cutters to be disgorged as spaghetti.

Carefully we laid out the freshly made pasta onto another table where it had to remain for twenty four hours in order to dry. Just as sufficient spaghetti had been made to fill one table, so the machine gave up the ghost and fell to the floor. The reason was obvious. I held up the machine to show Roxannie the width of the clamp was too large and pointed to the insufficient overhang of the table. There was just too little area to secure the machine properly. Roxannie's rumbustious turning of the handle, as if it was a barrel organ, had caused the clamp to lose its grip. Unfortunately, the table had been made with the top not fixed on square.

"Oiki provlema," grinned Roxannie, pointing to my side of the worktop, which had a wider edge. With a grunt, she picked the table up and with effort turned it round, so the greater overhang was on her side. It would have been far simpler to have passed the machine over to her, but ours is not to reason why!

With machine now in place and firmly clamped, the manufacturing process could now begin in earnest. We knew Roxannie made pasta once a year, which was then stored and used throughout the winter. We did not realise exactly what this involved.

Soon, all the tables in the Kafenio were covered in laid out fronds of spaghetti - and still the dough kept on coming.

Soon all the chairs had been draped and then the freezer - until a small boy came in asking for an ice cream, whereupon all the spaghetti had to be removed. With arms outstretched I was the dummy who copped the lot. Soon I was festooned with pasta while the dear little mite leisurely compared the merits of an orange Rocket Booster to the creamy delights of chocolate Magnum. With steel blue eyes fixed coldly on the dallying child, and lips drawn tightly over my teeth I hissed, "Make my day, punk. Go for your Magnum." As I was dripping with spaghetti at the time, the effect did not exactly reach a Clint Eastwood level of menace. Finally the little angel made his decision and the pasta was again laid to rest over the freezer.

And still the dough kept coming.

After two hours of rolling dough, cutting it into strips, machining out the spaghetti and arranging it to dry, every conceivable surface in the Kafenio was now draped with long strings of pasta - from the top of the television, high up on its wall bracket, to a variety of trays on the floor.

Tourists calling in for a Coke, were handed two cans and glasses, dusted with flour and politely asked if they could take their drink outside. This they did most obligingly, for one thing there was nowhere to sit, and for another, they weren't exactly sure how they had come to stumble upon a spaghetti factory.

Finally we came to the end of the dough. There must have been fifty kilos of pasta hanging around - but Roxannie was not finished yet. She had twelve tourists arriving for dinner that evening.

Tiropitas were now the order of the day.

Taking a mound of flour, mixing it with water, olive oil, vinegar and salt, she made balls of filo pastry. Liberally flouring the one and only table in the Kafenio not covered in pasta, she took a wooden broom handle and proceeded to roll out one of the balls. Continually flouring and rolling, until it was so thin you could almost see through it, she cut the pastry into squares. There were two bowls by her side. In one was 'horta' and in the other was crumbly, homemade feta cheese. Spooning some cheese into the middle of a square of filo, she sprinkled on some fresh herbs and brought one corner of the pastry to meet the other, forming a triangle, which she then sealed. Eventually there were twenty filled with feta and the same number with 'horta'. Fried in olive oil they taste out of this world - especially the cheese ones, sprinkled with sugar or dipped in honey.

Roxannie's culinery delights have reached further than just the village.

While President Mitterand of France was staying at the Acadomie, in Kolimabri, he and his entourage arrived in Afrata one evening, to dine at the Kafenio. They had heard of the wonderous traditional rabbit stew, which Roxannie was famous for.

Impressed that someone of such importance should wish to sample her cooking, Roxannie was even more flustered than usual. Sitting at the Kafenio drinking our coffee, we had seen her dashing hither and thither as she ran to and from the kitchen. We were unprepared when she appeared with two live rabbits. She was undecided. Could we choose? What was our opinion? Which one? It was our job to select the animal which the President of France would be dining on.

This was not Sainsbury's where meat comes wrapped in cling film and arranged on a polystyrene dish. Holding up the squirming rabbits by their ears - one bunny was brown, the other grey - there didn't seem to be too much difference in size. Taking a deep breath, I pronounced judgement and pointed to the grey. With a grunt of agreement, Roxannie delivered a sharp rabbit punch and the animal fell to the ground - dead.

Within minutes the animal had been skinned and jointed. Fried in olive oil and garlic, it was then casseroled with freshly picked herbs, the animal's blood, skin of orange, virgin olive oil and other secret ingredients which could well have been skin of newt and eye of bat. The end result was a thick, rich, aromatic stew. A dish fit for a King - or, in this instance a mere President.

Mitterand enjoyed his meal, shook hands with Alekos who had played waiter for the evening and gave Roxannie a kiss on both cheeks, remarking it was the finest rabbit he had ever eaten. He said nothing to me, the one who had personally selected the finest rabbit.

Over the next few years, as the stamp of so called progress has made its mark upon village life, Alekos and Roxannie have decided to add a few modern refinements to the Kafenio.

The first change was the WC. This was a tiny little hut, without a roof, which stood outside the Kafenio.

The original loo did not have a cistern. Consequently, when it came to flushing, you had to use the hosepipe, conveniently hung on a hook. The village water presssure is rather high and many an unfortunate tourist has emerged dripping wet, suffering from blow back, after having turned the tap on full.

Michylie was asked to modernise this edifice with a sink and flushing loo. Eventually a brand new toilet, complete with ceramic tiles to wall and floor were fitted. There was still no roof, but this was a minor matter. After all, there were no tourists during the winter when it rained.

One evening, shortly after the grand opening of the new loo, we were having a quiet drink with Michylie, when the door burst open. There stood his mother angrily wielding a broom as if it was a spear. Unleashing a tirade of abuse at her son, she made to lunge at him. Michylie was quicker off the mark, knocking over the chair he was sitting on, in his haste to avoid the punishment which was obviously coming his way. The more she shouted the more Michylie laughed. Round and round the Kafenio they went, Roxannie waving her broom, Michylie almost on his knees with laughter.

Apparently Michylie had had a lamb with him before coming into the Kafenio, and not knowing what to do with the animal, had locked it in the loo for safekeeping. Obviously the lamb was not housetrained - or rather, perhaps it was, because it had used the new facilities!

Modernisation of the Kafenio did not stop there. New double glazed doors were fitted and white ceramic tiles were laid over the old concrete floor. Then came the final piece de resistance - a new kitchen.

One day, remarking on the huge pile of building blocks, sand and cement, stacked haphazardly outside the Kafenio, Roxannie put a finger to her lips and whispered that we must not tell anyone. With a pronounced stage glance from right to left, to make sure we were not being spied upon, she confided she was having a new kitchen being built. We couldn't understand what the secrecy was all about. Surely the vast pile of building supplies stacked outside, sort of gave the game away!

Over the next two weeks a building gradually began to take shape, First the foundation - the new building was going to be at least three metres by four. Originally Roxannie had used her own kitchen, but this was a thirty metres walk away. Now, the extension would provide more cooking space and involve far less walking with trays of food.

Soon all the walls were built up to window height. I was a little concerned at this stage. One crucial factor appeared to have been overlooked. Outside the Kafenio was a lemon tree, which stood exactly on the spot where the extension was being built. As the foundations were laid, so the lemon tree stayed, laden with fruit.

As the walls were built, so the lemon tree remained.

I asked Roxannie if she was keeping the tree for her new kitchen? It would be so convenient every time she cooked, just reaching up to pick a fresh lemon. No. This was not the case. The man with the small JCB was at another building site and despite his promises had not yet managed to bring his machine up to Afrata. Thus Michylie had no option but to build the kitchen with the tree still in place.

Eventually however the JCB did arrive and with careful manoeuvering and dexterity, the five metre tall lemon tree was dug up, and carried out via the kitchen roof to be planted outside Michylie's house, on the opposite side of the road.

Now, with building work completed and a remote controlled colour television installed, the Kafenio has become fully modernised. Although perhaps just a little of its character has been lost.

September 3rd is a great day in the Papatherakis house. It is

Alekos' Name Day. Traditionally more attention is paid to the Saints Day you are named after, than an actual birthday. For those unfortunates, like Roxannie, who aren't called after a Saint, then All Saints Day covers this eventuality.

Alekos shares the day with his grand-son, who is named after him and grand-daughter, Aleka. A great family party is held and, as 'adopted' Papatherakis', we are invited too.

We arrived at eight o'clock in the afternoon, knowing from bitter experience you can miss an awful lot by not being attuned to Greek time. Morning lasts until about three and afternoon begins sometime after five. In between, the greeting - 'heratai' is a sort of time warp - being neither morning or afternoon. Even at ten o'clock at night you are still being welcomed with a "kalee spaira" - good afternoon.

We wished Alekos all the best and joined him in a celebratory tskouthia. Roxannie was all the time running to and fro, making everything ready. Gradually all the family arrived.

From Athens came the eldest son Costas, with his wife and two children. From Chania, came the youngest son, Andonis with his wife, joined by Miropi, Alekos' daughter and her family. Across the road from the Kafenio - the shortest journey, came Michylie and Sophia, together with their children, Roxannie, Alekos and Georgio.

A huge table was prepared out in the open for all twenty of us.

Alekos proudly served his own wine - a potent brew with a kick like a mule. We all toasted him, Michylie's son Alekos and Miropi's daughter Aleka.

As we were about to eat, Costas produced a bouquet of flowers which he presented to his mother. Touched, with tears in her eyes, she lovingly squeezed her son's hand and was then struck by an awful thought.

"Apo pou agorases ta loulouthia, kako pethee - where did you buy these flowers from," she demanded?

Costas grinned. "Apo ena magazi stin Tavronitis," he assured her.

Her eldest son had a wicked sense of humour. He worked for Olympic Airways in Athens, controlling baggage handling. Apparently he had brought wonderful sprays of flowers into his office one morning, for the three women who worked there.

"Oh thank you Costas. They are really beautiful. Where did you buy such lovely flowers at this early hour," they asked?

"From someone at the airport," recounted Costas, "he didn't seem to appreciate how lovely they were and didn't mind at all, when I asked if I could have them for you."

"They are really beautiful. You must have spent a lot of money on us," the women enthused.

"Oh no. Not really," laughed Costas.

"You mean you didn't pay him for his trouble," one woman said, surprised.

"Well no, I couldn't," grinned costas. "You see, he was dead. The flowers were off his coffin!"

"Ahhhh!!!" and the women threw the flowers they were

holding, up into the air as if they were red hot. Amidst much laughter they scolded Costas as if he was a naughty boy.

" No Mother, I bought them especially for you."

The feast spread before us was appetising in the extreme. My craving for cheddar cheese is satisfied with a wonderful village dish called Stakka. It is not really cheese, but the cream from sheep's milk and best butter, mixed and heated until it simmers like clotted cream. Warm crusty bread, straight from the oven dipped into a plate of Stakka is an experience out of this world. Just the same wonderful taste as molten cheddar, dripping over toast. I could kill for it!

"Michylie. Cressi," asked Alekos, pouring me some wine and not waiting for a reply. With everyone's glass filled, a sound cut through all the conversation. Alekos banged on the table with his glass and toasted - "see yia." Everyone clinked their glasses together, all exclaiming, "see yia," in return.

Now. What to go for next? The Pilaffe? The Rabbit?

The Pilaffe is a rice dish and is another Roxannie speciality - simply rice, boiled in a rich, homemade chicken stock, lemon juice and butter. The rice absorbs all the flavouring and is cooked until the liquid is reduced and then served.

The fish looked good too. Mmmm. Cutlets of grilled white fish. Mind you, the fried pieces of cheese, I knew were also delicious. Decisions, decisions. In the end I opted for the roasted lamb. Great chunks of meat, with the skin browned and crisp.

With drink flowing, food never ebbing and the constant banter of voices to and fro across the table, the enjoyable evening sped by.

The Kafenio is a wonderful place - a centre for gossip, for laughter, even philosophising - but always for food and drink and the time to share with good friends.

CHAPTER 11

An Orthodox Approach to Life

Religion plays an important part in village life. When we first arrived in Afrata, we were continually asked what religion were we? While C of E is the religious placebo which most easily rolls of the tongue, a little more explanation was required in Afrata.

"Ah. Your Church in England, it is Orthodox?"

"No."

"Ah. It is Catholic, yes?"

"No."

"Ah. Protestant?"

"Well .... no."

On the first occasion I was asked, I attempted to explain.

"About five hundred years ago, the English King - Henry the Eighth .."

"Yiati enai ton okto?"

"Because in history, there had previously been seven Henries, he was called the eigth. We number all our Kings and Queens.

I presume this helps school children to know which monarch is which. There have been an awful lot of Henries, Georges, and Edwards. Anyway, this King Henry married six times."

"Yiati? Etan ena Muslim?"

"No. He liked his women and when he wanted a new wife to replace the old, he had two options. One was to wait until she died. The other was to divorce, but the Pope would not grant permission."

"Ah, Pope. Esaste tous Catholics?"

"No. We were, but not now. Because Henry started his own religion in order to divorce his wife, we all called ourselves Church of England."

"Ah, Protestant," they would nod to each other knowingly.

Not being allowed to worship because of the sexual exploits of a King, was beyond the villagers' comprehension. As if to put us on the path of rightousness, we were continually being asked to attend church services. However, these would invariably involve experiences just a little different from the somewhat restrained, conventional services we are used to in England.

The first time we were invited to church was in May. Thinking it was the local church, we were surprised when Michylie offered to drive us and we agreed to be ready and waiting for him at eight thirty the following morning.

Curch was church and we presumably had to dress accordingly. With Pauline in her finery and me in a jacket - I drew the line at a tie - we were summoned to the gate by

Michylie tooting the horn of his truck. With due reverence, he held open the cab door for Pauline to squeeze in beside Sophia.

I was waved away to the open rear of the vehicle to join the kids and an elderly couple sitting on upturned beer crates. With a viscious kick of momentum, the truck lurched forward with a 'G' force almost throwing me off my crate. The elderly lady, clinging to her husband for support, lost her grip and nearly ended across my lap, but battled gamely to regain her balance, only to defy gravity for a moment as the truck dipped and then rose out of the dried up riverbed on its way up to the village. Unfortunately, she rose when she should have dipped, and her bottom came down on top of her alloted crate with a great thump.

Reaching the village, several more potential passengers stood expectanctly by the Kafenio. Young and old leapt or crept on board. Soon all the seating arrangements were taken up and the less unfortunate had to sit on the floor, which still bore the heady traces of a cocktail from recent loads - cement, bags of goat's droppings, live sheep, dead sheep and horta.

Down the mountain we went, all leaning into the bends, all bouncing over pot holes, all swaying on the downward descent. The synchronisation was a joy to behold. Along the coast we careered, with the wind in our hair and the magnificent panoramic view before us. Soon, a long queue of parked cars came into view. The truck slowed and drew up by a wire fence, which had been rolled back, by the side of the road.

The more dishevelled of the passengers brushed themselves down and straightened their attire, before jumping off, or being helped down from the back of the truck. Ever thoughtful, one kind soul built a landing stage out of upturned crates to ease the embarkation of the ladies. Joining Pauline, with Michylie and Sophia, we made our way along a dried out riverbed into the mountains.

A honk, honk, behind, made us keep to one side as a pick-up truck rocked and rolled along the rough terrain. As the vehicle passed by, its load of worshippers bobbing up and down in the back looked as if they were playing on a mobile bouncing castle. Truck after truck passed, as well as old cars which had seen better days. It seemed likely all the shaking would cause vital parts to fall off and they would end their days there and then.

Eventually, after ten minutes walk, with women wobbling and tottering on their high heels, we arrived at the place of worship - a tiny cave set high up into the mountainside. In front were steps leading up to a concreted area surrounded by a low wall, which doubled as seating. We could see Alekos above us, in his best jacket and tie, lying fully stretched out on the wall. From this reclining position, he was regally dismissing complaining worshippers with an imperious wave of his hand. One man stretched out over a space where four or five people could sit, was greedy in the extreme, but Alekos was oblivious to the trouble he was causing. Seeing us approaching he shouted, "Ela, ela. Etho."

Jostling our way through the crowd, we reached our 'reserved' seats, while others, less fortunate, were left to stand. Sophia carried an overly large handbag, from which she now took a newspaper and proceeded to place it upon the concrete wall as if laying the table for lunch. Torn between offending our friends who were concerned for our well being, and the danger of having yesterday's news imprinted on our backsides, we elected to sit.

For the next half an hour we watched as the villagers made their way into the tiny chapel, inside the cave. Many carried candles, made from brown wax. Others brought loaves of bread to be blessed. The Papas welcomed each person. They in turn bowed and kissed his hand. At any one time, only a dozen people could squeeze in and there must have been at least two hundred people attempting to push their way in or out of the shrine.

A large table had also been set up in front of the chapel, which served as a further obstacle for the crowd to navigate past - and soon this was laden high with loaves which had been blessed.

Finally, as the last dozen people filed out, so a strong baritone voice echoed from within, soon to be complemented by a glorious soprano.

Through the archway came the Papas, in his richly embroidered and silken finery of gold, green and cream. In one hand he held a bible. In the other he swung a filligree ball on a chain, from side to side and back and forth towards the congregation, filling the air with the smell of incense. Behind came a tall, handsome woman in a beige silk suit and cream blouse - it was Roxannie! Together they sang the scriptures - one passage by the Papas and then another by Roxanie.

Throughout, the congregation shuffled and whispered, while below us the people who could not push their way up, chatted in small groups. The Papas addressed the worshippers, who, in unison, replied and crossed themselves. The service lasted for perhaps half an hour, whereupon the Papas turned and made his way back into the chapel.

This must have been a signal, for everyone made a grab

towards the table. I turned to Alekos, but he was gone. Hearing my name called, I looked round and there he was, a lone swimmer against the tide, emerging from the crowd triumphant, his body protecting a booty of fish and bread. Pushing his way through, he slapped a fish into my palm and filled my other hand with a great chunk of bread. With all the noise and confusion I could just make out the words, "tregeis. Eenai poli oraio - eat. It is very good!"

I noticed Pauline had politely declined, but if she thought she had got off lightly, she had another think coming.

From her vantage point above us, Roxannie was concerned that Pauline had not received any of the blessed bread. Like a silly mid-on fielding an accurate return to the stumps, a large piece of bread sailed through the air over everyone's head, accompanied by a shout of - "Poleena." With an instinctive reflex action, Pauline raised her arm to take the bread in a brilliant catch, that would have brought a Lord's crowd to its feet. However, this Lord's crowd was more intent on securing provisions for themselves.

The bread tasted sweet, with a smattering of sesame seeds baked into the crust and a hint of incense absorbed during the service.

The fish was another matter. It was the size of a sardine and thickly encrusted with salt, from head to tail. looking around I could see people holding their fish by the tail and banging it against a tree or a rock to remove the salt. Those in the middle of the crowd, without the benefit of natural resources, resorted to holding their fish in one hand, while two fingers pinched tight, in a downward movement, squeezed the salt off onto the ground. Once this had been repeated once or twice, the delicacy was now ready to eat. With head to one cheek and a tail to the other, I took a bite out of the middle as if it was a Big Mac. Unfortunately I obviously hadn't acquired the correct de-salting technique, for it seemed as if I had bitten into a solid block of salt, saturated with fish oil. A mouthful of blessed bread helped resurect my ailing taste buds - but what do you do with a half eaten fish in your hand? You can't put it in your pocket and I didn't wish to offend anybody, by dropping it on the ground. I could see Alekos and Michylie tucking into theirs as if there was no tomorrow and they both nodded to me in a manner which plainly meant - "isn't this good?" I nodded back - "poli oraio."

On making our way out, I turned, only to be jostled by the heaving crowd. At that precise moment disaster struck - or was it a miracle? My elbow was knocked sharply and the fish fell from my grasp. Unfortunately, it did not fall to the ground. Instead, the stout lady in front of me, who was carrying a large bag, would arrive home to find something a little fishy had occured!

As we descended the tiny steps to ground level, the jostling made me lose my balance and I reached out to steady myself against a huge boulder. It was then that fate took a hand. I had forgotten. Dozens of fish had been slapped against this rock and now most of the salt and scales had been transferred to my palm. I smelt my hand. Phew. Fish fingers.

My consternation was interrupted by an "ela, ela," at my elbow. Alekos was on the hunt for more sustenance. Dragging Pauline by the hand, he forcefully pushed his way through the crowd to an old man standing at the foot of the steps with an old sack held up to the passing congregation. Was this the equivalent of the collection tray? No. With a few words of greeting and thanks, Alekos dived into the sack to bring out several wedges of cheese, one of which he threw to me as I reached the final step. Handicapped by the bread I was still holding, I caught the cheese against my chest. "Bravo," grinned Alekos. It was hard and white and tasted a little like cheddar, but far more salty - or was this a flavour enhancement enriched from my fishy palm?

Still chomping, we stumbled along after him as he gracefully threaded his way down the rocky terrain to a waiting truck. "Ela, ela, he shouted over his shoulder. Breathless, we reached the truck to be met by a smiling Alekos, holding out two pieces of meat wrapped in paper napkins. Above him, a man was ladling great chunks of goat meat out of a large cauldron, and passing them down to eager customers. The meat was absolutely delicious, tasting a little like lamb.

The paper napkin also served to remove the cloying remnants of fish from my hand. However, I thought the spreading grease stain on my shirt from the cheese was beyond redemption. Not so. "Oiki provlema," said Alekos, seeing my concern. Taking a piece of blessed bread he rubbed at the stain. Hey presto, or should I say Hallelujah - the stain disappeared!

Having sampled all the culinary delights on offer, Alekos felt we should wait for Roxannie. Looking up towards the chapel, we saw her, looking a little concerned, talking to a chubby faced, middle-aged man with wiry grey hair. It was Nektarios. Later that day he was to have a massive heart attack. He was flown to Athens where severe hardening of the arteries was diagnosed and a triple bypass deemed the only option if his life was to be saved. Within a week he was flown to London and operated on - all paid for by Greek medical insurance. Thankfully the operation was a great success, apart from one or two hiccups of which you will hear later.

Suffice to say, the following year, when the annual service was held at the tiny chapel, all the candles brought by the faithful palled into insignificance. Like a Scotsman about to toss the caber, Nektarios arrived with the largest candle I had ever seen in my life. It was so large I was surprised he didn't suffer another heart attack - but so grateful was he to be given a second chance in life, that this served as a religious token of his belief and thanks.

Not every service we attended was as eventful, but always it was an enriching experience.

A little nearer to home, we were invited to a short service held on the roadside in Afrata. As you enter the lower village, on the right hand side, perched on the edge of the road, overlooking the tremendous view sweeping down to the gorge, stands a little shrine in honour of St. Yannis. It was here, early one morning, that we assembled.

The Papas arrived, having walked all the way up the mountain from the Monastery in Kolimbari. Despite the exercise of walking everywhere, the priest cut a portly figure, dressed in a working grey cassock, which billowed out around his ankles as he walked. He was not bald, but over the years his forehead had grown up to a hairline, which now disappeared beneath the hat he wore. A straggly, mousey beard, which in his younger days could well have been red, blessed his chin. Twinkling eyes smiled at the villagers as he called a cheery, "yassus."

After the short service, a table full of loaves was blessed and large pieces handed out to everyone. It was an altogether far more restrained ceremony, rather than the jubilant atmosphere at the service in the mountains. Although this time we suffered an interuption from tourists in a car, who mistakenly stopped, believing there had been some kind of accident. Ever friendly, one villager passed through pieces of blessed bread to them through the open windows.

As everyone returned to their homes, each clutching their bread, we were invited by Roxannie to join them and the Papas for coffee, before he made his return sojurn down the mountain. The Papas was a kindly man, similar to a respected old country Parson, who knows everybody by name and takes care to pass the time of day with all his flock. We all 'hoovered' away at our coffee - unfortunately Pauline had by now accepted this as normal etiquette and the impact I used to make now fell on deaf ears. However, I can still enjoy that frozen stare back in England, where social graces are not so accomodating.

The clock in the Kafenio struck ten thirty. With a start, Roxannie excused herself and went out to the kitchen. Thinking something was amiss I followed her to see whether any help was needed. She showed me a plastic bag and explained that every single day of her life, at ten thirty, wherever she was, she ate holy bread. The bag contained a gold crucifix and a piece of loaf about the size of a biscuit - but the bread was green with mildew. This was no matter. Once every year she saved a piece, blessed by the Papas and thereafter would religiously eat a few crumbs every day. She maintained by doing this she would always enjoy good health. Going by the penicilin, I didn't doubt this for one moment.

After a pleasant half hour chatting, the Papas decided he must depart, as that afternoon he had to visit some parishioners in a village on the other side of the mountain. For the sake of a fifteen minute drive, the least we could do was to make the offer of driving him back to Kolimbari. He accepted most gratefully. Squeezing his bulk into the tiny front seat of our Fiat Panda, he did his best to crouch down in order to keep his hat on. Sitting hunched up, his hat of office jammed tight against the roof, we set off. On reaching the church at the top village, he asked whether we could stop for a few moments as he had some urgent business to attend to.

Five minutes went by and as it was so hot, we left the car and looked into the tiny graveyard. It was evident from all the gravestones - both simple and ornate, that several families had spawned the whole of Afrata's population. Roxannie had told us that her parents and two other couples in the lower village had had thirty four children between them!

A new grave stone in magnificent engraved grey marble belonged to our friend with the new house. Her photograph, set into the stone, smiled out to us. It struck us as a delightful tradition and a touching testimony to someone's life. Altogether different from the rather sad edifices we are used to, which have no bearing on the personality of the body long since departed.

Our reflective thoughts were broken by the slamming to, of the church door. Returning to the car, the Papas explained that his elder brother who lived in Canada, was extremely ill and he had prayed for his swift return to good health.

Arriving at the Monastery, he thanked us for our kindness and wondered whether we would care to come inside for a drink. Parking the car off the road, we walked the twenty metres to the stone portico entrance, set into a high wall of limestone. On the old, wooden doors was emblazoned a schoolmasterly demand - Dress with modesty. No shorts to be worn. I often felt this was a contradiction in terms. If you are wearing shorts, did you have to take them off to gain entrance? However, we were correctly dressed and could therfeore disregard this sign with impunity.

Entering the courtyard beyond the doors, it was as if we had stepped into the past. The quadrangle housed numerous shrubs and flowers and the greens and bright colours softened the ancient honey coloured walls surrounding us. Steps led up to a walkway running around the courtyard, where doors and windows could be seen, to rooms which no doubt housed incumbent monks.

Ahead, with doors open, beckoned the Monastery chapel, ornately styled and crowned by a dome of terra cotta tiles. In the shade stood the Papas. "Ela," he beckoned and we dutifully walked to where he stood. Turning, he led us into the room behind. Hanging on the walls inside, faded sepia photographs of Abbots taken over the last one and a half centuries, watched us enter. After the brightness outside, the interior was really dark, but after a few moments, our eyes gradually became accustomed to the gloom. I could see that the room was some sort of study, but a study that appeared to be of the same age as some of the photographs. It was furnished with ornately carved, dark wooden furniture and an old desk was totally covered with yellow papers, discoloured as if by age. Also on the desk stood a decanter with three small crystal tumblers and a plate of turkish delight.

The Papas poured us a tskouthia and explained that the Monastery had its own vineyard and olive groves and made all its own wine and pressed its own olives. Why, even the delicious confectionery had been made there and contained succulent almonds from their own trees. The fire from the pure spirit was an excellent companion to the sweet turkish delight. Thanking the Papas for his hospitality, we made our way out into the sunshine and back into the twentieth century.

The little chapel, near our house, is used twice a year - once in

May and again in August on its name day - the day of St Steven. To the tolling of the solitary bell perched high above the chapel, the whole village is summoned. The track from the house to the church is totally crammed with cars and trucks parked at every angle. Tourists arrive to find an impasse, while those returning from the beach are held prisoner in the gorge until the hour long service comes to an end. The culinery delights at this service are not so much in evidence, although as always there is much bread.

This is the one time of the year that our church going involves a mere two minutes easy walk. A blessing after the other theological escapades we have enjoyed. However, these are but mere trifles when it comes to a real pilgimage - our next sojurn.

CHAPTER 12

Pilgrim's Progress

August 29th is the day of St. Yannis - St. John.

Exicitedly Roxannie told us it was a wonderful feast day and, as true Afratearnie, we were expected to attend. Following instructions, we duly arrived at the Kafenio wearing our regulation, walking shoes, at the appointed time of two in the morning - by now we were well into Greek time and realised this meant just after lunch!

Roxannie and Alekos were waiting by their old Peugeot. The maroon monster was dented and battle scarred and must have been twenty years old if it was a day. With great formality, Alekos held open the door to the rear seats and we settled ourselves in the back. Roxannie put the column change into gear and pushed the accelerator down to the floor. For a second or two the reviving engine threatened to shake the car to pieces. Then, with countdown reached, her foot was removed from the clutch and we were launched like a space shuttle - leaving clouds of smoke in our wake.

As we passed the village shrine doing about Mach 3, our test pilot crossed herself as a sign of respect, ignoring the fact that a sharp bend was fast approaching. Without the benefit of two hands on the steering wheel we careered round totally on the wrong side of the road and almost on two wheels. This was no matter, when Roxannie was out driving, the news spread like wildfire and children, old people, goats and sheep were all kept indoors until it was safe to venture out again.

Roxannie had personalised the interior of the Peugeot with a beautifully made lace doilly, which ran fully across the top of the dashboard. Complementing this, anti-macassars were draped over the top of both front seats as if they were armchairs and, hanging from the driving mirror, an assortment of crucifixes jangled continually like a wind chime. Stuck onto the dash were pictures of all the Papatherakis children and one of Roxannie and Alekos, taken when they were in their twenties.

Alekos could not drive, but, as co-pilot he was responsible for in-car entertainment. No sooner had we started then the radio was turned on, and to the sounds of traditional Cretan music, accompanied to the beat of Alekos' hand clapping, we took the road out of upper Afrata and across the mountain. The views were breathtaking. Through the tiny hamlet of Stratigos we sped and out over rough terrain, where there was no road, only a dirt track. It was obvious Roxannie had travelled this way many times before, as she knew each pot hole personally, swerving continually, this way and that, in an attempt to steer round them. After some fifteen minutes of being thrown from side to side and bounced up and down, we were glad to arrive at our destination - Rotherpou.

Coming off the mountain track onto a relatively made-up road, was like travelling on a rubberised carpet, it was so smooth and quiet. Pulling off from the large village square, Roxannie parked with great aplomb down an adjacent side street.

While Rotherpou is much larger than Afrata, there are no shops, apart from three or four tavernas and kafenios, which all face onto the square. As in Afrata, the villagers depend on the travelling shops, which call each week. With loudspeakers blaring, announcing the wares they have for sale, one van will sell items of clothing, another vegetables and yet another fish.

Being villagers and following centuries of tradition, most houses keep chickens and rabbits, as well as a few sheep and goats. Therefore a supply of meat is always assured - although this is only eaten maybe two or three times a week.

From the car we walked back towards the square, where perhaps a dozen or more people stood. Alekos was weighed down by a huge carrier bag - it was the ever proverbial bread to be blessed at our final destination. After ten minutes of waiting, everyone began to shuffle restlessly, but finally the purpose of our wait came into view - a cream van. As usual, Alekos took command and he shepherded Roxannie and Pauline to the passenger side of the vehicle. A few succinct words and the three of them squeezed into the driver's cab.

I had drawn the short straw yet again!

The rest of us were left staring into the black hole of Calcutta. There, in the gloom, synonomous with every pilgrimage to church, lay the stacked beer crates. A sensitive English soul, trained to queue and allow ladies to go first, is at an immediate disadvantage when it comes to establishing terratorial rights over your own beer crate. My mother would frown, but there was no way I was going to sit on the floor of the van and personally experience every rock and pothole we were surely going to travel over.

Thus it was that in an instant I shed nearly fifty years of ingrained consideration of others and fought tooth and nail for ownership of my own crate. Like a victorious gladiator, I claimed my prize and sat on it, while others around me fought for theirs. With everyone pushed in, the driver slid the side door shut. The only light came through two tiny windows in the back doors. Ventilation was zero. Outside, the sun beat down a glorious thirty five degrees. Inside, already we were beginning to cook. With a lurch we were off and I could see we were leaving the square, but when we left the village and reached the mountain track, dust totally obliterated the view.

I passed the time of day off and on with my fellow in-mates. The lady who was perched next to me, wanted to know how many children I had and what were their ages? She came from Rotherpou and her family had lived there for generations. She had six boys and two girls - all good children. I guess nowadays television has become a much maligned form of birth control, compared to the days of no electricity. That was only thirty years or so ago, when bed in winter provided the only option for keeping warm.

After fifteen minutes the air had become virtually non-existent. I began to feel like a skewered souvlaki as the temperature reached boiling point. Finally it became so unbearable that a lad defied certain death by sliding open the side door. Boulders sped by as the van lurched along. The boy came perilously close to falling out, only to be clung on to by his extremely large mother. If he fell, her bulk was more than sufficient to plug the gap in the door.

After half an hour, we were still hot with the sun baking down on us, but with the increased ventilation, we could at least breathe. However, the red dust which was now blowing freely into the van covered everything. As I faced the open door, I soon discovered that speaking allowed a thick film of gritty dust to settle on my teeth. Staying quiet was a far better idea. Eventually, after what felt like ten days travelling through the Sahara, voices could be heard. We could make out figures and people waved to us as we chugged past. Finally we reached our destination and ground to a halt. My crate and I had become very attached to each other and we found it difficult to part company. Sweat and dust had virtually super glued it to the back of my bare legs. Leaving momentoes of a bright red 'AMS' and a 'TEL' tatooed on the back of each thigh, I joined the rest of my dust encrusted pilgrims.

The 'Royal Party' came around from the front of the van, having travelled in veritable luxury and just laughed at my appearance. They even had the gall to complain the ride had been bumpy!

We were on a small plateau surrounded by rocks where dozens of cars had been parked and people milled around expectantly. Our 'bus' was now in the process of doing a thirty three point turn in the confined space available, in order to return and cram in more unfortunate souls from Rotherpou. In front of us stood a refreshment van, of the sort you would expect to see outside a football ground. It sold soft drinks, 'burgers and hot dogs and looked decidely out of place for a pilgrimage. "Ela, ela." Alekos was eager to get the show on the road and we dutifully followed him through a wide gap in the encircling rocks.

Once through the, an amazing sight met us. There, way way below, at the foot of the mountains surrounding it lay a verdant green plain. Thousands of people, looking from this distance as if they were but a column of ants, were all focussed on moving towards a single point - a tiny church huddled in the centre of this green oasis. Roxannie told us twenty thousand or more people, every year, on this special day, made the pilgimage to the tiny church of St Yannis.

Impatient pushing from behind made us move from our

vantage point and start the descent. The pathway down was rocky, but not too difficult and the mountainside was a delight, studded with yellow gorse and countless bushes of thyme, sage and oregeno. For the herbs, a hot summer sun and the effect of our legs brushing by was a heady combination, impossible to resist. Each plant released its potent, fragrance, wafting away on the breeze to unite with its neighbours' and filling the air with an aromatic headiness as we made our downward descent.

As we walked I noticed there were many girls who were making the walk without wearing shoes.

"This was a tradition - a good luck omen," explained Roxannie. "If they make the pilgrimage to the church in their bare feet, they will be married by next August."

I think I would have preferred to remain a spinster.

The climb down was indeed enjoyable, although with the numbers of people there, it was a mite congested. Alekos was soon getting impatient. Being used to walking the mountains he preferred to go from A to B by the shortest route possible.

"Why walk twice as far on the zig zag track? That is only for city people," he snorted, and off he went as agile as an old mountain goat.

After half an hour, we made it to the bottom of the mountain to be met by Alekos, sitting on a rock for all the world like a garden gnome. He had a broad smile on his face. For the last ten minutes he had been sitting there, looking up at the human chain descending the mountain. Calling me over, he motioned me to sit down. "Vlepees, kako pethee - see, you naughty boy ..." and he pointed to where the chain broke, some twenty metres above us. Like a naughty schoolboy he was enjoying the sight of ladies having to stretch their legs out, to reach a metre drop. Invariably there was a flash of thigh and occasionally a glimpse of underwear. He screwed up his eyes, silently whistled and waved his hand in a tight circular motion from the wrist - graphic Cretan for "corrrrr." Roxannie caught him out the corner of her eye and made to give him a clip behind the ear. Too nimble for her, the seventy three year old ducked away under her hand laughing.

The walk across level ground was easy on the legs after the steep climb down. As we approached the tiny stone built church, we could see there was a large tree beside it - taller than the chapel itself. Roxannie explained that when St. Yannis arrived in Crete, he made his way to this very spot and plunged his wooden staff into the soil, decreeing that here was to built a place of worship. The stick eventually sprouted and grew into the huge tree, which was the only one of its kind on the island. Bearing in mind the distance and the difficulty in travelling to this spot, I felt the original Christians must have had a perverse sense of humour.

Outside the church a Papas addressed the milling crowd. He stood on a stage built on scaffolding and behind him, perched a large loudspeaker which boomed out his voice. Alekos and Roxannie entered the chapel to light a candle and leave the loaves they had brought.

Their pilgrimage completed, they emerged after five minutes to lead us beyond the church to where hundreds of people were milling. Like a car boot sale, without the car boots, stalls were set out on rocks. On one, plastic toys were being sold. On another, there were flip-flop sandals. Presumably these catered for the girls who hoped to be married within the year. Above all, it was food and drink being offered for sale. Little primus stoves heated chestnuts, corn on the cob, or skewers of souvlaki. The more entrepreneurial spirits had staggered down with tons of equipment. There were tables and chairs laid out, while in their midst, great cauldrons bubbled away over fires.

We sat down at a table and from his capacious bag, Alekos drew out a loaf, a huge chunk of cheese and cans of beer. We were going to have a picnic! Out came a knife and four spoons - was there going to be a sweet too? No.

With an "ela, Michylie," I followed him over to one of the cauldrons. While Alekos renewed old acquaintences, I ventured a look into the pot. Two eyes gazed wistfully back at me, out of a sea green bubbling liquid. As if inquisitively, another pair of eyes rolled over to look at me, before the simmering liquid dragged them down to hidden depths. Dragging himself away from old friends, I could see that Alekos had acquired four pottery bowls.

"Afto eenai poli oraio, eh Michylie," he asked, picking up a ladle from the table nearest him. I wasn't sure whether the contents of the cauldron were 'poli oraio', but in the foodline I followed the maxim, nothing ventured, nothing gained - I was willing to try anything once. Laying the four bowls down, Alekos plunged the ladle into the boiling cauldron. The contents from the first dredge were not considered worthy. The second however was deemed of sufficient quality to be poured. For several minutes this careful sifting and judging continued until sufficient ladles had been poured to fill the bowls. Fortunately, there was not an eye to be seen. Overseeing Alekos' judiscious pouring I realised the eyes were not out on their own, but were still very much attached, set into skulls which were now boiled a deathly white.

Carrying the bowls back to the ladies, I did not tell Pauline that what we were about to eat was stewed goat's head. She is a little sensitive where some food is concerned. More careful examination of my steaming bowl identified pieces of potato, chunks of meat and slices of onion. The smell was delicious - and the taste heavenly. What we were eating was a true Cretan gastronomic delight. Coupled with the crusty bread Alekos had brought to dunk in the soup, this was a meal never to be forgotten. In fact, so magnificent was it, that I had to have a second bowl to see whether it was as good as the first. It was!

Eventually, with the rock I was sitting on beginning to make a lasting impression, it was time to go. More and more people were still arriving and it was already gone six. Apparently thousands stay the night and there is a festival atmosphere that lasts the whole night through and into the following day. However, we had to go.

As we began to make our way back, a glance up the mountain ahead of us, presented a daunting prospect. Stocking up with some cans of soft drink, we began our ascent.

The going was made all the more slower, because we were now sharing the worn track with others still coming down. Babies were being carried upon fathers' shoulders. Old ladies dressed in black, effortlessly made their way down. Stretching for a foothold, the occasional, tantalising glimpse of a pop sock could be seen. Occasionally a true pilgrim would pass, hobbling along on the stones. Knowing how painful it is on walking just a few metres on a pebbly beach, let alone down a whole mountainside, you had to admire the poor girls' asperations. I wondered whether they were starting from scratch in the marriage stakes and had no potential beau in tow - or did they have a possible partner already ensnared and this was designed as the final nail in his coffin, from which there was no escape?

Soon I forgot the other people. The exertion up the mountain was beginning to take its toll on my lungs. Half an hour crawled by and we still seemed a long way from the top. Knowing the conquest of mountains relies on safety first and teamwork, I roped myself to Pauline, by taking her hand. She wasn't puffing like me, but her legs were struggling. I looked up. There was Alekos and Roxannie striding out for all the world as if they were on a Sunday stroll.

Sherpa Tensing and I struggled on for another twenty minutes, before we collapsed onto a conveniently smooth looking rock. Below us, there were still crowds and crowds milling around. The church looked so small from up here. Looking further across to the mountain range beyond, they were beginning to change in colour to a golden orange.

Time was fast approaching to make a move. With horror I looked up. Someone surely must have moved the mountain top - it looked further away than ever.

Pulling my guide to her feet, we staggered on. Gradually it became dusk and still people were making their way down. Finally, after nearly an hour and a half we made it to the top. Unfortunately we did not have a Union Jack with us to mark our achievement. Looking down at the scene below, for one last time, the mountains were now black, framed by an ever deepening golden halo. Sounds of people descending to the plain below could be heard and a thousand lighted candles could be seen. Tiny pin pricks of light, diamond sharp in the cool night air led down the mountain in single file, to burst out across the plain below leading to the bonfires which had now been lit around the church. It was a triumphant sight.

Like two pixies, Alekos and Roxannie were waiting for us either side of the pathway, as we arrived at the top - journey's end for our rasping lungs and leaden legs. It was now extremely dark and we still had the drive back to look forward to. The time was eight thirty and it was still as busy as when we had first arrived that afternoon. Cars and trucks were busy manouevering this way and that, their headlights scything through the night like demented searchlights.

Alekos led us to a large open truck. It was obvious he did not have any pull with this particular driver, because we were all to travel in the back together. The proverbial beer crates were at the ready, but this time merely serving as a ladder for embarkation. Stacked three high with a base of six, step of four and a final two step, we climbed to the top to discover the seating aarrangements consisted of rows of metal chairs, all roped together.

Not realising how high we were, I stood up and my head disappeared. I've never been accused of having my head in the clouds, but this was the real thing. With the cold night air, clouds were skimming the mountain top. It was an eery experience. When standing, all I could see about me was a grey, swirling mist. Like a descending diver, I bent my knees and beneath the surface of the grey world, vision returned. I was not the only one fascinated by the experience, for behind me stood three headless bodies.

Sinking onto my cold, metal seat, we waited for just a few minutes more, as other passengers boarded and the truck became full. Finally, with a lurch, off we trundled towards Rotherpou.

The journey back seemed quicker than our arrival in the afternnon - perhaps because I could breathe and wasn't being boiled alive. The trip proved uneventual apart from having to reverse fifty metres, when we came headlong into a convoy travelling towards us. After a few choice Cretan expressions, tantamount to, "if you do not allow us to proceed, you will force me to adopt an altogether more agressive attitude." our driver gave way. He had obviously decided he had little clout when confronting the superior forces of four trucks and two cars.

Fifteen minutes later, we came across a lone goat standing in the middle of the track. Agressive hooting did not make any impression. Perhaps it was deaf? However, a two ton lorry bearing down on it, without any intention of stopping, proved the animal was most definitely not blind. With a bleat of resigned acceptance, it ambled off the road to be missed by a hair's breadth.

The lights of Rotherpou beckoned. It proved a welcome sight. My back was aching from being continually thrown against the back of the metal chair, as the driver unsuccessfully navigated a million potholes. I was cold after all the exertion and with it, muscles which I never knew existed, and those which I did know of, but had never had cause to use in years, had meanwhile all set solid.

The night however, was still young.

Reaching the square, we could see during our absence out in the wilderness, tables and chairs had been set out to feed the five thousand. Alekos explained that a famous bouzouki player was arriving and there would be dancing, food, wine, ohhh - a night to remember. Where does the man get his energy from, I wondered?

Like children out with teacher, we dutifully followed the pair to a table set on the edge of what was going to be the dance floor. Continually, Alekos would greet a cousin, uncle, or nephew. One old man stopped by our table, dressed in traditional Cretan style, with baggy trousers tucked into calf high, black shiny boots, a black shirt, bristling white moustache and a fringed head scarf worn over the forehead. Alekos explained that Petros was the eldest son of his father's brother. We shook hands all round. Drinks were called for. Tskouthia. We thumped the tumblers on the table - "see yia" - and everyone clinked glasses, in the traditional toast "health to you".

It also sounded suspiciously like a Glaswegian threat - 'see you, Jimmy'!

Baskets of bread were brought to the table as well as dishes of horiatici salata - village salad of tomatoes, cucumbers, peppers, onions, olives and a big chunk of feta cheese, sprinkled with fresh herbs. Along with this came carafe after carafe of village wine - a high octane, sweet wine like a turbo charged sherry. And then, in case the level of alcohol became so great that stomachs required further fortification, all in a rush we were served platters of fried potatoes - grilled fish and grilled meat.

More and more people arrived, both those from the pilgrimage and lazy ones who merely set out from the local villages around. With the succulent food washed down with the wine, the crowd was both cheerful and noisy. Occasionally a little too much so. Gunfire cracked and echoed around the square, the sounds bouncing off the mountain backdrop above the village. The reaction was immediate as a pom, pom, pom filled the air. Applause and cheers of appreciation followed. Only to set off another gun toting guest, to even more applause.

In the villages every man owns a gun and it is traditional to fire off a round or two at festivals and weddings.

Accidents may occasionally occur, but in the main it is just an overexhuberant way of letting off steam! It certainly makes for an exciting atmosphere, not knowing whether you are going to stay alive long enough to finish your meal.

The time was now ten thirty and a hush spread through the proceedings, as a tall man, wearing black trousers, embroidered waistcoat and an immaculate white shirt, strode to the far end of the square where instruments had been arranged. As he picked up the bouzouki, the night reverberated to a salvoe of gunfire. People cheered and clapped, for this was what they had been waiting for.

For an hour the crowd were held spellbound, listening to the maestro playing traditional folk songs of Crete. The magic of his performance evoked the very essence of the island's folklore, as supple fingers danced over the strings and notes tumbled over themselves to be heard. The soulful melodies were instantly recognised, ingrained in the memories of both young and old. People began to clap and sway to the lilting rythmns. Others sang softly to themselves. Roars of appreciation went up as each Cretan song was played, the evocative music wafting through the air - ancient sounds which somehow echoed across the centuries to draw the mind back to that of yesteryear. With a rush, our thoughts returned as the last notes faded away on the breeze and the maestro waved goodbye. As he stepped down to a cacophony of applause, cheers and gunfire, three more musicians appeared.

The concert was over and now it was partytime - Cretan style.

An old Cretan dance tune started the proceedings. First the

plaintif sound of the Lyra, complemented by the more urgent Bouzouki, with its fast double beat of notes rising and falling to the insistent melody. Drawn like a magnet, young and old alike took to the floor and danced to the haunting music. I glanced at Alekos. Despite all the noise, he was fast asleep.

"Aleko," called Roxannie, shaking his arm. He was awake in an instant, and in one lithe movement, was immediately up and on the dance floor, with arms outstretched and fingers clicking in time to the rythmn. His feet lightly traced intricate patterns in time to the music as he weaved this way and that. Roxannie lost no time in joining him. Under the captivating spell of the haunting rythmn, the years fell away and it almost seemed as if the couple before us were in their twenties, as they danced so perfectly together.

In England there is a great divide between the elderly, who prefer waltzes and quick steps and the young who dance to rock. In Crete there is a valued continuity with the past. Both young and old have a bonding, cemented by the family, which is passed down through each generation like an Olympic flame. There is a fierce Cretan pride in maintaining these traditional links with the past. The happiness and enjoyment showing on everyone's face made it a privilege to be part of a community at one with the world.

This somewhat reflective mood was abruptly broken by Afrata's action man calling me to dance. Why do people do that, when they know you are going to make a real pratt of yourself? Yes. That's probably all part of the fun. Mentally I left the chair. Physically my legs and thighs remained. Rigor mortis had set in. My legs were dead tired and totally seized. There was no tolerance being shown and, with a grimace, I shuffled out to my torturer a broken man. Gradually, my pain racked body gained some semblance of movement and a certain mobility returned.

With eyes fixed trancelike on Alekos' feet, our arms locked shoulder to shoulder, I attempted to follow his steps. Unfortunately, by the time my brain had issued instructions to my feet, the moment had passed and I would be moving in totally the wrong direction. Alekos, kind soul that he was, stopped and then started again on the beat. However, I am not blessed with great natural rythmn and I was a half beat slow off the starting blocks. My memory also leaves a lot to be desired and without being able to remember the steps, within seconds I was again all at sea - much to everyone's amusement. However, reinforced by the wine, I eventually began to get the hang of it - or perhaps the potency of the village brew only made it seem as if I did.

The haunting sounds played on, sometimes slow, but invariably fast, much to the obvious delight of everyone. Over a period of hours Alekos and Roxannie gradually ran out of steam and finally collapsed onto their chairs. It was time to go. I looked at my watch. It was nearly two in the morning and I knew Alekos had to be up and out by six for the sheep. Hundreds of people were still there - and likely to be so until dawn, but bidding our farewells we walked to Roxannie's car.

The drive back across the mountain to Afrata proved uneventful, except for the glorious view of shimmering moonlight upon the sea and twinkling lights all along the coast to Chania, way, way in the distance. Arriving back at the Kafenio, we said our goodnights and Pauline and I set out down the mountain path. Tip toeing past darkened houses to the last corner, we made our way down the steep descent and through the olive groves to home.

There was no doubt. Going to church here, was just a mite more strenuous than we were used to. Yet it had been a super day - and night!

CHAPTER 13

Mission of Mercy

Thankfully, after being struck down after the church service with a massive coronary, Nektarios' triple bypass operation was a complete success, although his English surgeon recommended he take life a little easier and prescribed an early retirement. With the healthy mountain air and peaceful surroundings of Afrata, he and his family stayed in the village throughout the summer, rather than the hustle and bustle of Chania.

As prescribed, he dutifully walked the five kilometres and swallowed an asprin every day. Some days he looked fit, on others very pale and his one time paunch was now very much reduced, after his illness. He was a short man with receding grey curly hair, a prominent forehead and would invariably smile quizzically, because of poor eyesight. Being from the town, he was always dressed in smart casual clothes and when the weather was hot, sported a wide brimmed straw hat, making him look like Mr. Magoo attempting to impersonate Clint Eastwood.

One day, he looked extremely poorly and despite the hot weather, felt very cold. Athena, his wife, fussed about him, always anxious if he was below par. No matter how concerned she was, he was not going to call for a doctor.

Athena was tall, slim and several years younger than her husband. Before her marriage she had been a hairdresser, but since then had dutifully spent all her time at home bringing up the children. She had dark brown hair and a ready smile, with a tendency to shyly avert her gaze when speaking.

The following day, in the mid-afternoon, when everyone in the village took a nap during the heat of the sun, I was awoken by a voice from the garden.

"Michylie, Michylie? Signomi."

It was Athena. At last the previous two days had proved too much for Nektarios and he had capitulated, finally agreeing to visit the hospital. Unfortunately one thing scared him more than seeing the doctor - Athena's driving.

Quickly Pauline and I dressed. Athena had walked down to us and therefore to save time, the three of us drove back in our car. When we reached the house, Nektarios was already sitting on the verandha, with a blanket wrapped round him. He managed a weak wave and looked at our small Fiat in a derogatory fashion.

"Eenai polli mikro aftokinito. Then nomizo na eenai asfalos
it is a very small car. I don't think it is safe," and he gave me the key to his Toyota.

This was twelve years old, but looked immaculate as it had just been resprayed. Nektarios was helped into the front passenger seat and Athena and Pauline flipped up the driver's seat to make themselves comfortable in the back. The car had been parked in the sun all day and as soon as I sat in the driving seat, I wound down the window to let out the build up of heat.

"Oiki,oiki," complained Nektarios,"kreo, kreo - it's cold."

I started the car and checked the mirror, adjusting it to the correct position.

"Oiki, oiki. Then vlepo - no, I can't see," and the patient twisted the mirror back towards him. "Tora borro na vlepo ta aftokinita appo pisso - now I can see the cars behind."

Was this a back seat driver, or was this a back seat driver? I was the one driving. He was the one looking!

Off we went. First, second and up to third gear.

"Ciga, ciga - slowly, slowly," commanded my driving instructor.

We crept along at twenty miles an hour. I glanced at Nektarios. He was grey and sweating with the heat. Inside, the car was stifling. Surreptitiously I opened my window, only to be told to keep it closed.

Coming out of Afrata onto the mountain road, I was conscious of something on my head. Whatever it was, began to spread down over my ears. In all the heat, the roof lining was coming away. Athena leant over me and patted the lining back into place, grumbling that this always ocurred now they had had the car resprayed.

Suddenly Nektarios made a grab for the wheel. Fearful he would steer us over the cliff, I chopped at his arms to break his grip. He punched me in the shoulder and reaching under my arm repeatedly sounded the horn as we approached a bend. Not wishing to be responsible for him having another heart attack, I said nothing as he shouted at me toalways sound the horn as a warning at every bend to avoid a possible accident.

The fact the bend was not a blind one and I had plenty of visibility was of no consequence. Begrudgingly I tooted our way into the open, cliff hugging road, where we began to pick up speed. Tantalisingly going into top gear, a barking, "ciga, ciga," put me back into third.

Like a theatre safety curtain descending at the interval, my vision was becoming impaired. Athena came to the rescue and patted the lining back into place again.

As we crept down the mountain, Nektarios hooted at a parked car, every stray goat and every curve in the road, should there be the faintest possibility of another vehicle lying there in wait ready to crash into us.

Way down below I could see Stavros phut, phutting up the mountain on his melon truck - a turbo charged lawnmower, which resembled a cross between an invalid carriage and a schoolboy's homemade cart. It was loaded to the gunwhales with 'horta'.

I could see Nektarios becoming more and more edgy as this life threatening danger approached. Finally, he could stand it no more and in desparation ordered me to stop and pull into the mountainside for safety.

There we sat for five minutes. The suspense was killing. Finally we heard a chug, chug, chug and there, round the corner came Stavros at a steady five miles an hour. As he passed, a full five metres of wide open space lay between us! He waved a cheery "yassus," with a bemused expression on his face. Why were four people waving to him like demented fish in a bowl? Recognising me in the driver's seat, the answer was obvious. Ah. An Englishman.

Like fish, we silently mouthed,"yassou," in return.

Inside, things were hotting up. Perspiration was running down the face of everyone. Nektarios still complained of being cold and turned up the heating control to maximum. The roof lining came down in sympathy. Athena patted it back up again.

As we carried on, the steep descent made the car go faster.

"Ciga, ciga," ordered my co-pilot.

Seeing that her husband was looking decidely unwell, Athena leant forward and instructed, "grigora, grigora - quickly quickly."

"Oiki. Ciga, ciga," countermanded Nektarios, and an arguement began to flare. Fortunately we were saved by the curtain. Athena was temporarily diverted by having to pat up the lining, which was festooned over my head, threatening navigational visibility.

Still cold, Nektarios turned on the booster fan to maximum.

We had only reached the bottom of the mountain at Kolimbari. Would we live to see Chania, or would we melt?

At the crossroads out of the village, I made many abortive attempts to turn left, but was curtailed by Nektarios holding on grimly to the handbrake. He was determined to wait until there were no cars within a kilometre of the immediate vicinity, before allowing us to venture across. Eventually the coast was deemed to be clear and off we went, with an impatient, "ela, ela," as if it had been me holding things up.

With the temperature inside the car now resembling a sauna, the adhesive properties holding the roof lining finally gave up the ghost. It was now a continual game of pat-a-cake and time to improvise, if we were to reach Chania. Asking Pauline to check whether there were any unbreakable items in her handbag, I devised a solution. Being fairly tall, I used the bag as a cushion and, sitting bolt upright, jammed my head against the roof. This appeared to solve the problem, but caused some discomfort when the car went over a bump.

We were getting along famously now, with my radar operator advising me of potential hazards enroute.

He was still cold. We were all stifling. However, we had just driven through Agia Marina and now there was only a few more kilometres to go. Fortunately, with it being mid-afternoon, the roads were quiet and we made good progress.

Unfortunately there seemed to be a problem with the innovative solution. My ears began to tickle as the dreaded roof lining began to descend like some loathsome creature from the Black Lagoon. My head was pinned against the roof and my bottom jammed to the handbag. With furrowed brow and ears of roof lining growing ever longer down my face, it must have seen from the outside as if the car was being driven by a bloodhound.

Now we were in Chania, we had another problem to contend with. Traffic lights. Nektarios believed he had a sixth sense, for as we approached each set on green, he was convinced it was just about to change and would instruct, "ciga, ciga." Consequently we approached each junction at snail's pace, with the handbrake held in readiness for an emergency stop. This only served to further endanger the convoy of hooting vehicles behind us. Conscious of this fact, I changed up to third, like a test pilot putting his plane through its paces. A "ciga, ciga," from air traffic control brought me swiftly back into line, with a squeal of brakes as the red pick up from behind nearly ended up in front.

Worried in case an aggressive pedestrian may stray off the pavement, I was now instructed to stay well into the middle of the road for safety reasons. Consequently, with heavy traffic coming towards us, the pick up behind, could only overtake on the inside. This he proceeded to do with continued hooting, offensive gesticualtions and a shouting of oaths, all aimed at the idiot responsible for such poor driving.

In effect, me.

His Cretan temper now enflamed, Nektarios wound down his window to give vent to a suitable reply. We all gasped as fresh air, albeit tinged with benzine, reached our grateful lungs. From outside it seemed as if a radiator had burst. Clouds of steam escaped all around Nektarios as hot air from inside, met the cooler air outside. Fuming that his rude, yet pertinent graphic gestures had been interpreted in the mist as mere waves of friendship, Nektarios felt he should revert to the role he played best - that of patient.

I was grateful the patient hadn't asked me to put forward a point of view on his behalf. Sitting on my handbag, head jammed against the car roof and sweat and ears running down my face, did little to create an aura of intimidating menace.

Finally, like a circus parade, we arrived at the hospital in a fanfare of hooting cars.

Wishing her husband to see the doctor as quickly as possible, Athena was desparate to get out of the car. "Michylie, grigora,

grigora, parakalo."

As I bent forward to reach for the door, I was conscious of a weight on my shoulders. From a bloodhound, I had undergone a metamorphisis to a blushing bride. The whole roof lining had casquaded down to create a plastic veil. Worse. Due to the heat built up in the car, the lining was now stuck to my head. Fears of ripping it off like a huge great sticking plaster made my eyes water just to think of it. Gingerly I pulled the lining up, slowly separating it from the hairs on my head.

Athena was by now getting more agitated. Seeing my situation, she then urged Nektarios to get out of the car. Grey and sweating, he groaned as he attempted to open the door. "Grigora, Michylie." It now seemed I was the centre of attention. Like a sadistic nurse, Athena began to pull at my 'veil'. Ahhhh. The first hairs decided to stick it out with the lining, only to be pulled forcibly from my skull.

Pauline then leant over and six hands attempted to free my head. For nearly an hour Nektarios had been urging me to slow down. Now it seemed he wanted me to hurry up. Finally, with only a few yelps - I was extremely brave - all but one tuft of hair remained glued. With the patient now slumped almost comotose against me, Pauline decided a more drastic course of action was now called for. Following instructions I pressed upwards, enabling her to reach under my nether regions to retrieve her bag. Fumbling inside she triumphantly held up a pair of nail scissors. Without so much as a by your leave, or an anaesthetic, she just cut off the offending hair, as deftly as if she was Sweeny Todd.

Now we were moving.

With the three of us out of the car, we rushed round to the

passenger side to remove Nektarios. In our haste I forgot the bald patch I now sported on the top of my head, as we half lifted, half dragged him out of the car. Prepared to carry him up the hospital steps, I thought I heard a low murmur. His eyes were closed, his face had a pallor of death and I bent down, to hear clearer what he was struggling to say. I could just make out a faint, whispered last request. "klisto to aftokinito - lock the car."

No person of authority, or anyone else come to that, did we encounter on our way through the entrance, and up three floors in a lift to where there was a seated waiting area. Athena and I then proceeded to discover the whereabouts of a doctor, or the very least a nurse, in this Marie Celeste of a hospital.

In agressive Greek style of firing first and asking questions later, we opened the closed doors facing us. The first was empty. In the second was a half naked man lying on an examination table. On being asked whether a doctor was on duty, he confirmed he had been lying there for half an hour and was still waiting. The third door revealed another empty room, but we struck lucky with the fourth. Nektarios' doctor was examining a patient.

"Tha perimenoume exso," Athena informed him, to which he gave a curt nod.

Five minutes elapsed before the rather limp wristed doctor emerged to ask Athena and Nektarios to come into the third room.

After a quarter of an hour, the doctor reappeared and in a gutteral German accent, but in perfect English said, "how do you do? I am afraid se pharmacy in se hospital iss closed end ve shall hev to go to ze, er, shop - pharmacy - in ze town. Nektarios iss perfectly alright, but iss suffering from a mild reaction to his operation. However, we require some medication to help him through se next few days." Still wearing his white coat, billowing out behind and shiny shoes tip tapping on the tiled floor, he minced down the corridor waving us all to follow.

Outside, in keeping with his social position, he indicated the back seat would be occupied by the patient, supported either side by the women. Satisfied with the arrangement, he lolled across the passenger seat, pulling out a cigarette holder from inside his voluminous white coat he wore over a bright yellow waistcoat.

"Don't vorry. I do not smoke. I jest need, how you say - se substitute," and he proceeded to load the holder with a cigartette. "Com. Ve go now to se pharmacy."

It was a luxury to change gear and steer the car where I wished. In the mirror, which I now had all to myself, I could see the face of Nektarios. He looked a little more amenable now.

"Here pliss. Here iss ze pharmacy. Zey vill prepare se medication for you. I live just round se corner. Thank you pliss for se lift," and with that he got out of the car and bade us farewell.

Athena went to collect the prescription and then all I had to do was drive home. I sighed and gritted my teeth in readiness for all the abuse likely to come my way from both inside and outside the car.

Slowly I pulled away. From first, into second and up to third.

Travelling at a heady twenty miles an hour, we soon attracted a convoy. As the hooting started, I began to cringe at the prospect of the slow drive back, the danger of jay walking pedestrians, and the threat of parked cars - not to mention the odd stray goat.

Suddenly, from the back came an instruction. "Grigora, grigora." Now that he wasn't dying, Nektarios wished to return home quickly!

CHAPTER 14

Moonshine

After the grape has been trod and wine for the following year safely casked, the concentrated purple residue of grape skins, pips, leaves and stalks are scooped into large polythene bags. Ingredients to create the spirit of Crete - tskouthia - Cretan moonshine.

Each village on the island takes pride in their local spirit, which is strictly controlled by the authorities. In Afrata, Ellias and his family have held the license to distil tskouthia every year for generations past.

With the summer gone and the grey skies of winter upon us, Alekos and I borrowed Roxannie's car to drive the short way up to the top village. Two grandads out on the town set forth with a cheery wave to our spouses as we left to enjoy a morning out on the razzle. A permanent choke and a short clutch made the Peugeot leap up the road like a demented kangeroo possessed. Parking below the two Kafenios, we walked through the tiny alleyways between the houses up to the home of Ellias. Immediately, the pungent smell of grapes wafted towards us on the breeze. The chatter of voices drew us to the back of the house, where the October chill melted as we stepped through a curtain of heat and entered a scene repeated from centuries past.

Seated around a table were four men, chatting to an old lady, dressed in black. Behind them, like a great edifice was the still, perched high above a roaring furnace of white hot fire which spat and sparked. Everyone bid us welcome and immediately small glasses were brought out to us by Ellias' wife, accompanied by a dish of salted peanuts in their shells and another of freshly baked biscuits. Michylie, Alekos' son waved a cheery welcome. He had been working at the still since before dawn and his curly dark brown hair and bushy Cretan style moustache glistened with perspiration. "Katsi, katsi," he beckoned, pulling up two chairs.

It was obviously a time and a place to sit and chat - for where else could you find a place so warm and friendly, with a limitless supply of drink on tap? An old boy with a mop of unruly white hair, twinkling eyes and an equally unruly long beard, introduced himself as Periklese. He was dressed in the traditional Cretan style of black shirt and jacket, voluminous trousers tucked into his calf high boots and across his lap lay a knarled and twisted walking stick.

"Eesai Germanika," he asked? To roars of laughter I replied,"Bah! Oiki! Eemai Afratiano - No. I am from Afrata!" We all toasted each other and downed a tot of the freshly distilled spirit.

The old lady was about to leave with her lunch. She was very tiny, with a hand-embroidered apron around her waist and wire framed spectacles peering out from beneath a black scarf, knotted beneath her chin. Earlier that morning she had brought in a casserole of chicken pieces and potatoes. Pouring olive oil, lemon juice and freshly picked herbs over the meat, she had left the pottery pot on top of the furnace where it had slowly simmered. It was now cooked to perfection. The chicken was browned and the potatoes had absorbed all the natural flavours. With hours of slow cooking, the sharpness of the lemon and the richness of the oil had combined to give the dish a delicious combination of flavours.

With a towel she picked up the hot casserole from the top of the furnace and bid us farewell with a cheery, "yassus."

"Kali orexi," we called - "good appetite," and we raised our glasses, but they were empty - time for a top up! Alekos took the yellow plastic beaker from the table and walked over to where the still dispensed its booty - in a metal container set into a pit carved out of the solid bed rock. The fiery liquid was still warm, but as smooth as smooth. "See yia," we toasted and another tot went down the hatch.

As always talk now turned to politics - the villagers were staunch socialists with the Pasok Party, which had only just been re-elected. Consequently in their judgement taxes would soon be reduced and the money earned from olive oil and oranges would be much higher. One of my new friends aired his views. He was a cheerful man with a ruddy, round face. Thin tufts of fair hair sprouted from the top of his head and his knarled hands continually jabbed and cut through the air to give added emphasis to the points being made. Satisfied with the results of the elction and the advantageous changes which would soon take place, he commiserated with the state of politics in England and asked, "eenai o Major kalos - is Major good?" I clicked my tongue and jerked up my head in true Greek style. "Oiki - eenai ena malaka." They roared with laughter and my bosom buddy, who had asked the question, slapped his thigh at this bawdy description. He grinned hugely, to reveal the one solitary tooth in his head.

"Ela," instructed Ellias to Michylie, waving him towards the fire. The last drop of spirit had been distilled. Now it was time to work and fill another barrel.

Ellias had a round moon face, covered in white stubble, to match the luxuriant growth on his head. A sweat stained, striped shirt was almost impossibly stretched over his sagging stomach, beneath which hung loose denim jeans, rolled up above his ankles. To finish off this vision of sartorial elegance he wore a pair of designer trainers.

He wobbled over to the still, which was set beneath a vast, clay tiled canopy extending out from a wall of rock. Stout wooden beams, blackened and charred from the heat, supported the roof, which afforded protection should it rain. Beneath this canopy, a stone mound had been built, sooted and steaming from the open fire raging in its belly. Ellias climbed the stone steps to the summit, where the metal edifice was secured - a huge inverted round bowl, similar in shape to a blacksmith's anvil. With gloved hands, he grasped the handles which protruded like horns from the metal beast. With eyes like black buttons staring out to sea over the rooftops below, he crouched, concentrating on calling upon every ounce of effort he could muster. With a strangled cry, he twisted the still and pulled. Up it came in a hiss of steam. Ellias stood there triumphant, like Hercules with the world on his shoulders.

"Bravo, bravo." Watching this trial of strength was thirsty work. Time for another tot. "See yia."

Michylie, his jeans burnt from the sparks and boots stained with soot, shovelled out the glowing embers of half burnt logs from the red hot stone furnace. Before cleaning the still, everything had to be cooled down. Buckets of water were poured over the area. The air was filled with white steam, pungent with the smell of heated grape remains. Out of the swirling mist, Michylie could be seen with Ellias, on top of the furnace, shovelling the fruit residue out of the cauldron, which was set directly into the stone, its flat base in contact with the white hot embers. Continual dousing wrought great jets of steam into the air, like some primeval creation. Eventually the job was done. On all fours, Ellias crouched over the cauldron to be sure it was completely clean. Satisfied, he struggled to his feet and ambled down the steps to rest and gulp down three glasses of water.

We had another tot in sympathy with all this strenuous work. "See yia."

Alekos explained that tskouthia was indeed a wonderful creation. Mothers rubbed it on the gums of their babies to relieve the pain of teething. The nagging itch of an insect bite could be chastened by an application of this wonderful brew. Colds too could be cured. Rubbed on the chest, it would soothe a cough. During sleep wearing a woollen scarf doused in tskouthia helps make breathing easier. It was indeed a miracle cure.

We were now at the funny stage, prepared to laugh at anything.

Alekos recounted a favourite joke concerning an old man waiting for a bus, with a live turkey under his arm. Not having much money and knowing he would be charged a fare for the turkey, he stuffed the bird down his trousers. To be sure the bird could breathe, he undid his trouser buttons.

On the bus, he sat next to two women. Not interested in listening to their idle chatter, he held up his newspaper to read. The ladies continued talking and one offered the other some nuts. Suddenly a swelling became apparent in the old man's trousers, but he seemed oblivious of the fact as he continued to read. There was now a large bulge. Both women looked at it extremely impressed. "Have a nut," said one to the other, offering an outstretched hand. Before she could take one, the turkey's head and neck shot out rigid, pecked a nut and vanished back into the trousers. The women looked at each other agog. Finally one said, "I've seen them in all shapes and sizes, but that's the first time I've ever seen one eat nuts before!"

Amidst all the laughter, Michylie and Ellias had returned to work, placing briars of herbs in the cauldron to prevent sugar from the vines sticking to the inside. Michylie then emptied four huge containers of grape remains into the metal crucible. Crouching on top of the furnace, on all fours, Ellias looked for all the world like a giant bulldog, his tongue lolling out with the effort of pressing down on the purple mound. With a grunting and a straining, he jammed the contents tightly into the bowl until it could take no more.

Finally he called to Michylie who brought over a cask, raised it up over the open still, and poured in about ten litres of village wine. Sniffing the contents, his eyes closed, Ellias ran his mind over years of experience and pronounced himself satisfied that all was well.

Carefully the cauldron was mated with the top of the still. Using his finger, Ellias spread a concoction of ground ashes, flour and water around the join to seal it absolutely airtight. Carefully he also sealed the joint between the trunk extending from the still. This was connected to a coiled pipe fixed inside a fifty gallon oil drum of ice cold water from the mountainside.

Although the furnace had been raked out, the retained heat was still so fierce that when Michylie rolled two great logs into the grate, so they immediately burst into flames. As the searing hot air engulfed us, so we toasted the fire with another tot. "See yia!" - and we all clinked glasses.

Aristotle, the chubby chap with the solitary tooth, philosophied that life was hard, but he had a solution to help make things easier - if only I would help him. Being lifetime friends since our first drink together that morning, an intoxicating air of bon homie was warmed by the fire and the tskouthia. I replied - "of course."

"Then when you return to England, find for me a widow woman. One who has plenty of money. One who misses having a man," and his toothless grin spread from ear to ear. "Then all my problems will be solved."

"They are just about to start, old friend," laughed Alekos, pointing over his shoulder.

"Aris. Ela." It was his wife. We all toasted him goodbye. "See yia."

Alekos leant over and beckoned me to come closer. Looking about him to ensure our privacy - which was non existent - he whispered confidentially, "Aris was an old shepherd who had spent too long with his sheep. He had a problem. A big problem. His 'pouli' had flown its cage and was now of little use to man nor beast."

From now on I always thought of my drinking partner as the omnipotent, impotent shepherd.

By now Michylie and Ellias had joined Perikles, Alekos and I sitting around the table. The wicker seats on the rickety old chairs had begun to bite a pattern into my backside and I shifted uncomfortably. Perhaps I was a novice. Everyone else appeared to relax comfortably, be it on an upturned crate, or a chair like mine.

We reflected in our own thoughts as before us the furnace seared white hot, heating the metal crucible to a tremendous temperature. Within the still, steam given off from the grapes was being drawn along the trunk connected to the coiled pipe, where cold water caused it to condense into alcohol. At the base of the oil drum, a pipe extended above a pit. In this hole, hewn out of the solid rock, stood a twenty litre cannister. A large wire strainer and a white muslin cloth filtered any sediment, as a drop of tskouthia dripped every half second into the container below.

The colour was crystal clear, the taste was clean and pure - the natural spirit of Crete is tskouthia.

With one last tot - a "see yia" - and two legless grandfathers said goodbye to friends, each carrying a flagon of the precious liquid to be consumed at leisure, later. Linking arms, we leant on each other to keep upright down the steep alleyway. Once on level ground, Alekos showed me how to dance down the middle of the road. With arms outstretched, linked to each other's shoulder and Alekos singing at the top of his voice, two lighter men on their feet you couldn't wish to see.

As we gracefully zig zagged our way down to the lower village, Alekos became a little tired. We took a detour into the little playground, midway between upper and lower Afrata. There Alekos sat on a swing and within seconds had nodded off. Seeing a flash of reflected light way above us, I shook Alekos awake and grabbing him by the arm, we stumbled back towards the road. A car was coming. It was tourists. Two grandads flagging down two helpless German ladies says much for their confidence in travelling in such a wild part of the country. It was probably because there was no room in the road to pass that they stopped, rather than the sheer animal magnetism of two sozzled old men. With difficulty we clambered into the back seat of the Fiat Panda. The two buxom frauleins looked at each other as if to say, "what on earth have we done," and off we sped to the Kafenio, some four hundred metres away.

Tumbling out of the car with very pronounced bows and shouting "dankershern," and "efharisto," we waved the two women, "auf wiedersein."

Roxannie came out of the Kafenio to see what all the rumpus was about, just catching sight of our two lady friends as their car turned the corner, never to venture this way again. She frog marched us both inside and sat us down. "Who were those women? What were you doing in their car? Where have you been? And Michylie - where is my car?"

We had forgotten. It was still parked at the upper village. I looked at Alekos for help. He was fast asleep. It seemed a good idea.

CHAPTER 15

Reflections

Like a Mother Hen I walk my handkerchief estate each morning to see which new bloom is flowering. I tut tut to myself on finding the damned badgers have dug more holes during the night. At the end of the drive, beneath the canopy of vines, the drip, drip, of the irrigation line to the olive groves signifies the start of the working day. I lean over the gate and the phut, phut, from Stavros' melon cart can be heard as it comes round the bend. An "ela,ela - ne, ne," heralds the approach of Alekos as he calls to his sheep, shepherding them down to their pen. "Baa, baa," they go, leisurely grazing as they walk.

And then silence.

Except it never ever is really silent. Concentrate and there is the distant caw, caw, of a hawk, way up in the blue, blue, sky. The constant taca, taca, of cicadas in the olive trees is an invisible sound which you banish from your mind, like the tick tock of a clock. It's always there, but rarely listened to. High in the mountains which form the backdrop to our village, the tinkle, tinkle, of bells can be heard as goats leap from one impossible crag to another.

The Greeks have a perfect description of Afrata - 'eacie heare' - perfect peace.

The house is now finished. The garden is a picture. New

challenges await us in Afrata - an old stone cottage to rennovate - perhaps a place for people to stay awhile.

Ela - come. Like us, fall in love and enjoy a lasting affair.

One of the savage dogs of Hades keeping goats - and unsuspecting tourists from straying past

Somewhere, lost in the olive groves, is our house

The day we first discovered our new home.

Pauline contemplating whether we should make an offer

Not quite an English country garden.

Pauline doing a little painting.

Me giving the 'fornos' a rub down after its first baptism of fire.

The archeological remains of a cess pit, circa 1985 - now transformed into a sun terrace.

At last some semblance of order in the garden.

Sophia at our first coffee morning - de-scaling a fish!

Michylie and Alekos proudly showing me the gift they had brought - half a ton of sheep's droppings.

Steps up to the chapel and the track down the gorge.

Afrata's tiny cove - a pebbly beach and the clearest of clear water.

Alekos on Beethoven - *straight out of a Moussaka Western.*

Alekos leading his sheep astray.

The kafenio.

Alekos' giant 'pouli' - always an impressive topic of conversation.

Alekos and Roxannie.

Argirula and Nikos, Roxannie - a visiting shepherd - and Alekos.

Michylie and Ellias damping down the still.

Ellias, about to distil another brew of tskouthia.